Savage Farnum

Island Home stud of Percheron horses

Island Home Stock Farm, Grosse Ile, Wayne Co

Savage Farnum

Island Home stud of Percheron horses
Island Home Stock Farm, Grosse Ile, Wayne Co

ISBN/EAN: 9783337216702

Printed in Europe, USA, Canada, Australia, Japan

Cover: Foto ©Andreas Hilbeck / pixelio.de

More available books at **www.hansebooks.com**

ISLAND HOME.

OF

PERCHERON HORSES

―――――

ISLAND HOME STOCK FARM,

GROSSE ILE, WAYNE CO., MICH.

City Office, Campau Building, corner Larned and Griswold Sts.,
opposite the Postoffice, Detroit, Mich.

―――――

SAVAGE & FARNUM

PROPRIETORS.

DETROIT, MICH..
JOHN F. EBY & CO., PRINTERS, 65 WEST CONGRESS ST.
1887.

INTRODUCTORY.

In again presenting our Annual Catalogue, we take the occasion to call attention to some of the salient features of the subject treated—PERCHERON HORSES, their introduction to this country, and effect upon our stock.

It is now about thirty-five years since the importation to, and breeding of Percheron horses in this country began. With the prejudices and lack of knowledge, coupled with the generally favorable results from established systems of agriculture, it was slow work getting them before the public. It was not until experience had taught us that the breeding of the common mares of the country to Percheron stallions produced a horse adapted in an eminent degree to the wants of the farm, that Americans were convinced of their superiority over all other draft breeds. This created a demand for them unprecedented in the introduction of improved stock into the United States, while the profits are now greatly contrasted with general farming on account of the decreased remuneration derived· from the latter, caused largely by the great fertility and increased facilities of the West for the production of grain and beef as compared with the East with its high-priced lands, no longer relieved by dairy farming, which is rendered comparatively profitless by the manufacture of dairy substitutes. Ranchmen, as well as general farmers, have learned that they can place a three-year-old grade Percheron colt on the market at less expense and risk than is required to fit a steer for the shambles, and for the former they receive $150 to $300, while $60 is above the average price now realized for fat steers; and in the raising of pure-bred Percheron horses the profits are greatly augmented, as $1,000 is below the average price realized for three-year-old Percherons, including both stallions and mares. The present generation will see no decline in prices of either the grade or the full blood, as we have annually to produce upwards of a million of horses to supply the present demand, not to speak of the

increased population of the older sections and the development of the
various and extensive industries constantly being established ; while the
opening up of comparatively undeveloped sections of the South and West,
particularly the former, which is having a grand awakening to the merits
of Percheron horses as compared with the traditional mule, will largely
increase the number annually required.   In this connection we would note
the fact that we have sent five Percherons to one of the Gulf States alone
during the past autumn.

For the production of the million or more of draft horses annually sold,
upwards of fifty thousand Percheron stallions would be required, while
there are only about two thousand in service in this country.   No one, not
excepting the owners of rival draft breeds, will deny that the Percheron
stands pre-eminently above all others for this purpose, or that the value of
the annual product of draft and general-purpose horses would be doubled
by their use, an increase in the material wealth of the nation of no mean
proportions.   But, notwithstanding the establishment of extensive concerns
for the breeding of Percherons, we shall be obliged to depend upon impor-
tations for the bulk of the supply for many years to come.

The exhibition of the American Percheron Horse Breeders' Association,
held in Chicago in September last, was the crowning act in the drama, and,
with former and corroborating evidence, placed Percherons so far in
advance of all other draft horses that sensible men will have no further
doubts regarding their merits, and the propriety of breeding to horses
whose pedigrees are established by the records of the Percheron Stud
Books of France and America.   The show itself was greatly superior to
anything ever attempted in this or the old country, so much so that Marquis
de la Motte Rouge, Inspector General of the National Studs of France,
appointed by the French government to act as a member of the jury of
awards, remarked that "France itself could not, at the present time, offer
such an exhibit," but added, "Give us another year to bring forward
another generation of colts, and we will have a Concours worth visiting."

We are ready to admit that some good specimens of unrecorded draft
horses are brought to this country; but when a man buys a horse for breed-

ing purposes he should have some guaranty of what his produce will be, and this can be secured only through authenticated records of breeding. The importation of horses with no knowledge of their ancestry, with the attending pernicious results recognized by all breeders, must in the near future cease. In this connection we may quote from a speech delivered by the French Minister of Agriculture, M. Develle, at the opening of the National Concours at Nogent le Rotrou, in June last, the greatest exhibition of draft horses ever held in France. M. Develle said: "I must not forget, gentlemen, the reason of this *fete*. Allow me, therefore, to speak of the Percheron horses, and to congratulate you upon the successful efforts you have made to perfect and perpetuate this grand old race of the Perche, a race that is by far the best if not the only true race in France. Under the direction of distinguished men, the Societe Hippique Percheronne has become large and powerful, and to-day it is controlling and guiding the whole of the breeding district. The Societe possesses its 'Golden Book,' and after having seen this Concours I can say, without fear of saying too much, that the government means to give the whole of its power, influence and support to the Societe Hippique Percheronne, which, by its Stud Book, is keeping up the true breed." These utterances have a marked significance, and are particularly pleasing to the breeders of Percheron horses, coming from a man who controls the breeding of the country through the twenty-two government studs, sending out annually about one hundred stallions each; and they have a bearing not generally comprehended in this country, where the government takes no cognizance of such affairs.

SAVAGE & FARNUM.

Island Home Stock Farm, December, 1886.

ISLAND HOME STOCK,

While we have some choice Hambletonian horses, a fine band of Exmoor and Shetland ponies, a very choice young herd of Holstein cattle, and some French coach horses, imported last fall, and in which we expect to become largely interested the coming season, the main feature of Island Home is the importation and breeding of PERCHERON HORSES. Our this year's importation was selected by a member of the firm, Mr. H. C. Farnum, who spent the summer in France, and will be at the farm until the time for his departure abroad early in May. He took unwearied pains in its selection, accepting only animals of individual merit coupled with the most noted lines of breeding, a large percentage of them being prize winners in France as well as in this country the past season, while Romulus 873 (785) has taken more first prizes in one year than any horse in existence, notably that of the Paris Exposition in 1878, where he took first prize over all, and also a gold medal in addition as being a horse of especial merit.

Our prices are as low as the lowest for genuine pedigreed stock, and about as follows: For full-blood stallions, from $1,000 up; for full-blood mares, $600 up, and for grades, $300 up. Time will be given on approved paper when desired.

ISLAND HOME STOCK FARM

Is beautifully situated at the head of Grosse Ile, in the Detroit River, ten miles below the city, and is accessible by railroad and steamboat. The Island is eight miles in length and about two in width, the lower end being at the mouth of the river, while the north end, on which Island Home is situated, is nearly opposite the city of Wyandotte. The eastern channel of the river is about two miles wide, and constitutes the boundary line between the United States and Canada. It is the main thoroughfare for the vast shipping of the great lakes, there being always in view a number of vessels during the season of navigation; in fact, more shipping passes through the Detroit River, and consequently by Island Home, than any other point in the world.

GROSSE ILE

Is a popular suburban and summer resort. The boating and fishing are unexcelled. The scenery, with its many attractions, make it a most delightful place. It is accessible at all times by railroad. The Michigan Central (see time table on page 60) runs a special train for the convenience of the island people, many of whom are engaged in business in the city. Desiring a friendly intercourse with those interested in the improvement of the stock of the country, whether in our particular lines or not, we extend a cordial invitation to all to visit Island Home, where a friendly greeting awaits them. By calling at our city office, Campau Building, Detroit, or telephoning to the farm, visitors will be met at the steamboat dock or railroad depot with a conveyance. City office telephone, No. 1105; farm telephone, No. 51, 4 rings. If convenient, write or telegraph us when you are coming.

PLUVIOSE 3755 (683).

HISTORY OF THE PERCHERON RACE.

BY CHARLES DU HAYS.

AUTHOR OF THE DICTIONARY OF THE PURE RACE;" "TROTTERS;" "THE BOOK OF
THE RACES;" "THE MERLERAULL;" "THE HORSEB-REEDER'S GUIDE,"
ETC., AND THEN AS NOW OCCUPYING A HIGH POSITION
IN THE FRENCH GOVERNMENT

The following history is quoted from the work of the above author:

"Almost everything that has been written about the horse may be reduced pretty much to complaining that there does not exist a breed which unites, in an elevated degree, high moral or physical qualities; modestly seeking and teaching the means of obtaining such a breed.

"It is reasonable that such sentiments should surprise us, here in the heart of France, where, for a long time, a race of horses has flourished which may be said to fill the requirements proposed in every way.

"The proof of this statement is easy: a hasty sketch of the principal characters of the breed suffices to furnish it.

"To no ordinary strength, to vigor that does not degenerate, and to a conformation that does not exclude elegance, it joins docility, mildness, patience, honesty, great kindness, excellent health, and a hardy, elastic temperament. Its movements are quick, spirited and light. It exhibits great endurance, both when hard worked and when forced to maintain for a long time any of its natural gaits, and it possesses the inestimable quality of *moving fast with heavy loads*. It is particularly valuable for its astonishing precocity, and produces by its work, as a two-year old, more than the cost of its feed and keep. Indeed, it loves and shows a real aptness for labor, which is the lot of all. It knows neither the whims of bad humor nor nervous excitement. It bears for man, the companion of its labors, an innate confidence, and expresses to him a gentle familiarity, the fruit of an education for many generations in the midst of his family. Women and children from whose hands it is fed can approach it without fear. In a word, if I may speak thus, *it is an honorable race*. It has that fine oriental gray coat, the best adapted of all to withstand the burning rays of the sun in the midst of the fields—a coat which pleases the eye, and which in the darkness of the night allowed the postilion of former times to see that he was not alone—that his friend was making his way loyally before him. It is exempt (a cause of everlasting jealousy among the breeders of other races), always exempt from the hereditary bony defects of the hock, and where it is raised, spavin, jardon, bone spavin, periodical inflammation, and other dreaded infirmities, are not known even by name.

"This truly typical race would seem a myth, did it not exist in our midst. But every day we see, every day we handle this treasure, the munificent gift of Providence to this favored region, to cause agriculture, that 'nursing mother,' to flourish, and with agriculture peace and abundance.

"I need not name this breed ; every one, from this incomplete sketch, has recognized the fine race of steady and laborious horses bred in the ancient province of Perche (so justly entitled *Perche of good horses*), plowing in long furrows the soil of Beauce, and thence spreading itself over all France, where its qualities render it without a rival for all the specialties of rapid draft.

"That cool, restrained and ever fresh energy, that courageous patience of which the Percheron, every day, gives an example, dragging, at a trot, heavy loads, the weight of which frightens the imagination ; stopping short, both in ascending or descending ; starting off freely, and always without balking ; never sulking at his work or food, and fearing neither heat nor cold. He remains exclusively both the quick and mettlesome draft horse, and the heavy burden and express.wagon horse. He possesses superior strength, speed, docility, temper and honesty, and a complete absence of irritability. This is a specimen of Percheron qualities.

"Hence it is that all our provinces envy us the possession of the race, and even foreign countries seek after it with an eagerness amounting to a passion.

"The prices of these stallions have increased so rapidly in a few years that they have tripled and quadrupled. Accordingly, the possessors sold them. The administrative authorities, aided by the élite of the proprietors, endeavored, however, to hinder this immigration. They formed a stud-stable at Bonneval. Prizes were given at Mortagne, Nogent-le-Rotrou, Illiers, and Vendôme. But an end was arrived at contrary to what was desired. The prizes served as signs to the dealers. Perche was visited to buy first-class horses. What surer guarantee than the prize ?

"The breeder, who is ordinarily a farmer, not sufficiently rich to be beyond temptation, finds himself without strength, without resistance in presence of this urgent demand.

"The value of the Percheron is more evident than ever. It is this, among the serviceable races, which is called to the greatest fortune. His usefulness causes him to be everywhere in demand."

DESCRIPTION OF THE PERCHE.

"The Department of Perche is too well known to need a description here. We will limit ourselves to the remark that this region, which has become so celebrated for its fine race of horses, represents an ellipse of about 25 leagues long by nearly 20 broad.

"At the present time, enclosed in the center of the four departments, Orne, Eure and Loir, Loir and Cher, and Sarthe, the territory of Perche comprises the following divisions :

"1st—The district of Mortagne (department of Orne).

"2d—The district of Nogent-le-Rotrou, and a portion of those of Chartres, Dreux and Chateaudum (department of Eure and Loir).

"3d—All the western side of the district of Vendôme (department of 'Loir and Cher).

"4th—The eastern portion of the districts of Mamers and Saint Calais (department of Sarthe).

"It is the summit region of the middle portion of the vast plateau extending between the sea and the basins of the Loire and the Seine. It is here that the rivers Sarthe, Huisne, Eure, Loire, Iten, Höene, Braye,

Avre, Commanche and Percheron Orne take their source, springing up from the same plateau and crossing it on their way to the channel and the ocean.

"The country is, in general, uneven and hilly, cut up in every direction by small valleys watered by springs or small brooks flowing into the rivers above named. All these valleys, no matter of what extent, are natural meadows, and the most of them rich and fertile. The finest valley is that watered by the Huisne, which is second to none in France for length, extent, richness, and beauty of site. Here are situated Nogent-le-Rotrou, Conde, Regmalard, Boissy, Corbon, Mauves, Pin-la-Garenne, Reveillon, etc., etc.—all centers renowned for the beauty of their horses.

"The land is generally clayey, lying upon a calcareous subsoil of the secondary formation. Some portions are silicious; the high and hilly points always so.

"The Percheron country contains rather few meadows, in proportion to the total surface of the soil, and to this circumstance, probably, is due the superiority of its horses. Here the rearing takes place in the stable and the brood-mare is found under the hand of the breeder. Making use of her comes naturally to his mind. *He works* and *feeds* them well.

"Here, for many years, agriculture has flourished; artificial meadows are everywhere cultivated with success, and are necessary to produce the enormous quantity of fodder consumed by the number of horses raised.

"Among the plants for green and dry forage, clover first and then fenugreek, are the favorites of the Percheron farmer. He uses plaster and marl with care, and would tell you, should the opportunity offer, that it is through system and superior cultivation that Perche has been able hitherto to meet the large demands made upon her from the commencement of the present century, particularly for the last fifty years. He is, moreover, laborious and persevering. Disregarding the industrial arts, the glory of other districts, his true vocation, his favorite occupation, is cultivating the ground and raising horses, which he has practiced with zeal from the most *remote period.*

"Perche has a climate eminently favorable to horse-breeding. Under its influence the water is tonic and the food nutritious; the air is pure, bracing, and dryer than that of Normandy. The sea is farther off, and its influence, in consequence, is less felt.

"Everybody to-day well knows the influence of climate upon animals. No one now any longer doubts that it is to the sharp and healthy air of the Perche country, to its elevated hills, and to its atmosphere constantly renewed by the powerful ventilators of its valleys and forests, that this country owes the eminent qualities of its fine race of horses, which has won for it the right of displaying this significant title, 'Perche, the land of good horses.'

"The excellent care, the wise management,—exempt alike from pampering indulgence and from the harsh treatment which irritate the disposition, and from which the good teacher never departs in his intercourse with his pupils,—contribute a great deal to the success of the result."

ORIGIN OF THE PERCHERON RACE.

"The Percheron race comes from the Arab; but it is useful to know the causes which have separated it from the primitive type. How has it been modified? How has it lost the Arabian character, in which it must have been at first clothed? A large number of the French races have been even more profoundly modified, and have become abject, miserable, puny and misshapen. All equine races have been changed by the effects of climate, by the extinction of the feudal system, and by the inauguration of peaceful habits which have made an agricultural and draft-horse of the horse primitively used for the saddle and for war.

"From the time of the Roman domination, the horse in his oriental forms was particularly prized in Perche.

"Under the feudal rule, and inhabited by tenants ever at war, Perche must always have been an equestrian country, and the horse must have been there in every age the companion of man. He must have been really a first-class necessity. In those times of continued war and hostile surprises, what property was more movable and so easily taken to a place of safety? How glorious the possession of such noble coursers, and like the Rotrous, to own more than could be counted, as was proudly shown by the heraldic chevrons upon their broad banners, displayed from the towers of Mortagne and Nogent!

"La Perche, like all Christian countries, furnished, as is well known, her contingent of fighting men to the Crusades, and the chronicles cite several Counts of Bellesmer, Mortagne and Nogent, barons and gentlemen of that province, who, with many of their vassals, made pilgrimages to the Holy Land.

"The Abbe Fact, in his great work upon La Perche, cites in this connection a lord of Montdoubleau, Geffroy IV., and Rotrou, Count of La Perche, as having brought back from Palestine several stallions, which were put to mares, and the progeny most carefully preserved. The small number of the sires, their incomparable beauty and manifest superiority must have led to the *in-and-in* breeding so much deprecated by most breeders; but the qualities of the sires became indelibly fixed upon their progeny.

"The lord of Montdoubleau was, it is said, the most zealous of the advocates and breeders of the new blood, and, being the most zealous, was the most successful; hence it is that the Montdoubleau stock is to this day the best in Perche. The Count Roger, of Bellesmer, imported both Arabian and Spanish horses, as did Goroze, the lord of Saint Cerney, Courville and Courseroult; these are historical facts which have their importance. The fact is, the crusaders from all the French provinces naturally brought back with them more or less of the Eastern blood, which they had learned to appreciate on the plains of Palestine—but the truth is, it has not been preserved elsewhere; and that we in La Perche, after so many centuries, should be so fortunate as to be able to show the traces of it, should stimulate us to its careful preservation.

"We see toward 1760, under the administration of the Marquis of Briddges, manager of the stables of Pin, all the large number of Arab stallions that this establishment owned were put at the disposition of the Count of Mallart, for use at his mare-stables of Cocsme, near Bellesmer; and years after we find, at the same chateau of Cocsme, the grandsons of those old admirers of the Arabian with two Arab stallions, 'Godolphin' and 'Gallipoli,' both of which proved valuable stock-getters—both grey—which once more gave tone and ardor to the Percheron race in that vicinity.

"A direct descendant of Gallipoli, the renowned 'Jean-le-Blanc' of M. Miard, of Villers, near Sap, in the department of the Orne, etc., etc., placed alongside of an Arab, presented, notwithstanding his heavier and grosser form, analogies with him so striking that our curiosity was excited, and we did not rest until, after pressing inquiry upon inquiry, we discovered that he was descended from this famous Arab stallion. This horse, Jean-le-Blanc, was the most potent improving agent of Ouche.

"The Percheron of the primitive type has a gray coat like the Arab; and like him an abundant and silky mane, a fine skin, and a large, prominent and expressive eye; a broad forehead, dilated nostrils, and a full and deep chest, although the girth, with him as with the Arab, is always lacking in fullness; more bony and leaner limbs, and less covered with hair than those of other draft-horse families.

"He has not, it is true, the fine haunch and fine form of the shoulder, nor that swan-like neck which distinguishes the Arab; but it must not be forgotten that for ages he has been employed for draft purposes, and these habits have imparted to his bony frame an anatomical structure, a combination of levers adapted to the work he is called upon to perform. He has not, I again acknowledge, such a fine skin as the Arab, nor his prettily rounded, oval and small foot; but we must remember the fact that he lives under a cold climate, upon elevated plains, where nature gives him for a covering a thicker skin and a warmer coat, and that he has been for ages stepping upon a moist, clayey soil.

"In all that remains in him, we recognize a heavy Arab, modified and remodeled by climate and peculiar circumstances. He has remained mild and laborious, like his sire; he is brought up, like him, in the midst of the family, and, like him, he possesses, in a very high degree, the faculty of easy acclimation. He acquires this in the midst of the numerous migrations he accomplishes in Perche, the counterpart of those that the type horse makes upon the sands of the desert. A final comparison, which has not, as yet, been sufficiently noticed, is, that, like the Arab, he has no need of being mutilated in order to be trained, managed and kept without danger. In a word, the Percheron, notwithstanding the ages which separate them, presents an affinity as close as possible with the primitive horse, which is the Arab."

BREEDING BY SELECTION.

"Selection has long been practiced in Perche, and it has there produced for a long time the best results.

"Breeding by selection has numerous advocates, and, from all time, the best informed, the most practical men, have been unanimous in proclaiming that *blood is only preserved and improved by blood*—that is to say, by selection. It is easy and not expensive, inasmuch as the necessary subjects are always at hand; it is natural, inasmuch as its simplicity is apparent to every mind. And, if it does not bring the rapid results so pleasing to those too eager for profit, it is, at least, always sure. For, without giving at first exceptional results, it never fails in its effects, by reason of the affinity existing between the different individuals, and by reason especially of their perfect conformity with the climate and soil.

"If a horse is remarkable over all others in one of the three following ways: personal beauty, high qualities, or sureness of reproduction, go back boldly to his origin, and you will find yourself, at each step, face to face with close inter-breeding—that is to say, the reforming of a race by means of itself, the result of great qualities increased by drafts made at the source of a generous blood.

"The thoroughbred race in England, which has been formed but with a very limited number of primitive agents, and which, consequently, soon became consanguine, has, anew, and at two distinct epochs, absorbed, in every degree and repeatedly, the blood of two famous groups, represented, the first by 'Byerly Turk,' 'Darley Arabian,' and 'Godolphin Arabian;' the second by 'Matchem,' 'Herod,' and 'Eclipse.' At the present moment it maintains itself, thanks to a universal consangninity, and everything good which exists, by going back inevitably to these sole progenitors, now forms but one and the same family. Magnificent results have come from these alliances, and every day it can be proved that this blood has not degenerated.

"It is, especially and only, in the reproduction by family that a breed is formed. Consanguinity alone can form, in the beginning, a bond of cohesion and connection among the descendants of the primitive families. By it, alone, they acquire that great similarity of shape and adaptation to particular ends, that great ancestral power, which they transmit to their posterity, and which, even in a commercial point of view, gives them a superior value.

"It is the same in all breeding countries, and it has been shown (for proofs see the journal 'La vie à la campagne,' of November 30, 1863) that especially in Merlerault, the nursery of the fine French breeds, everything exceptionally good which exists, or which has existed, is the result of consanguinity—that is, 'in-and-in-breeding.'

"A stud book, recording its pedigrees, would not be out of place. This book would have the effect of concentrating the efforts of all the breeders, giving them a definite direction, and would give increased value to the breed, as is easily understood, for it is the surest of all the means of improvement and perpetuation of valuable qualities. It would drive off, forever, the defective stallions, and those corrupted with hereditary blemishes, as well as those coming from tainted families, which, I feel sure, would be refused a record in its pages. The prices of colts would likewise gain by this measure, the effect being a powerful impulse given to breeding."

COLOR.

"Formerly I liked the gray horse very much, and have more than once praised this color. But time has dissipated my illusions.

"Thus, while acknowledging my former preferences for the gray horse over the horse of a different shade, I am now very far from showing myself exclusive, and quarreling with the mass of enlightened persons who seem desirous of adopting the dark-colored coats. I only desire one thing, and that is, to save the Percheron race, and to preserve to Perche its prosperity and its glory.

"Let us occupy ourselves, then, seriously in looking up breeding stock of dark coats. The time to do this appears to me to have come. But where will we go to find them? Let us look about us and seek for this in Perche.

"If you there find under a dark coat, a fine Percheron, possessing all the qualities and specialties of the race, make haste, take him and color your horses. Sincerely, I give you this advice.

"Correct the defects of conformation, the imperfections of color, without weakening, without breaking up the harmony of the admirable qualities which have made of the Percheron the first horse of the age."

SPEED AND ENDURANCE OF THE PERCHERON.

"One of the qualities of this breed of horses, and which has acquired for them a universal reputation, is fast trotting while drawing a heavy load; but it would be an error to suppose that this ability to trot fast makes him an equal in every respect to the trotting breeds of the present

CLOVIS 5346 (6234).

day. The trotters draw very little, but have a long stride; and as regards mere speed, there is no comparison. The specialty of the Percheron—rapid draft—has its limits, and it is these limits that I wish to make known by numerous examples officially reported. What the Percherons do in the diligences, mail and post-coaches, is known to every foreign traveler, and it is useless to enlarge upon it. From one relay to another, drawing not less than two and often three thousand pounds, in all kinds of weather, over hilly roads, they make their three leagues an hour, and sometimes four, but this is *ne plus ultra*. What they do in the omnibuses, the world that visits Paris sees only to admire, and forms one of the greatest attractions of the Percheron horse to the observing stranger.

"We will now turn our attention to the trials made upon their trotting tracks. The places most frequented are those of Illiers, Courtalain, Montdoubleau and Mortagne; and in order to be impartial it is necessary to state that the tracks, all but the one at Mortagne, are plowed fields, hard in dry weather, but cut up in wet times, and that the track at Mortagne is badly located, having three steep inclines up and down inside of the mile, and the horses that have done best elsewhere have failed on this track, and it has taken a longer time to go the distance. To this circumstance is attributed the low averages made upon that track, but it also shows the courage of the animals. When a colt of two and a half years of age—there were several of this age—can accomplish his task by going two or three times around this track, there is a reasonable certainty of there being the elements in him for the making of a valuable horse. The most of the horses are trotted under the saddle, as their vehicles are of the most cumbersome character, and utterly unfitted to trot a horse in.

"The following shows the results of one hundred and eighty-nine matches officially reported, and two trials to prove bottom, likewise certified to, and will give an average of what the best Percherons are capable of doing.

"In order to be strictly impartial, the slowest and fastest time made is given :

"UNDER THE SADDLE—ONE AND ONE-FOURTH MILES—TWENTY-NINE RESULTS.

"The best two are those of 'Jule,' at Montdoubleau—time, 3 min. 50 sec., and of 'Godius,' at the same place, in 1857—time, 3 min. 58 sec.

"The poorest two results are those of 'Vidocq,' at Mortagne—time, 7 min. 37 sec., and of 'Lansquernet,' same place—time, 7 min. 48 sec.

"The average time of twenty-nine recorded trials is 4 min. 12 sec.

"ONE AND FIVE-SIXTHS MILES—THIRTY-ONE RESULTS.

"The best two are those of 'Vaillante,' at Montagne—time, 4 min. 38 sec., and 'Julie,' at Montdoubleau—time, 6 min., 14 sec.

"The poorest two are those of 'Mouche,' at Mortagne—time, 9 min. 18 sec., and of 'Biche,' same place—time, 8 min. 30 sec.

"The average time of thirty-one trials, 6 min. 40 sec.

"TWO MILES—FORTY RESULTS.

"The best two are those of 'Cocotte,' at Illiers—time, 6 min. 5½ sec., and 'Sarah,' same place—time, 6 min. 2 sec.

"The two poorest are those of 'Balzano,' at Illiers—time, 9 min. 40 sec., and of 'Renaud,' same place—time, 10 min. 30 sec.

"The average time of 40 trials is about 7 min. 20 sec.

"TWO AND A HALF MILES—SIXTY-FIVE RESULTS.

"The best two are those of 'Sarah,' at Langou—time, 7 min. 35 sec., and same at Mortagne—time 7 min. 40 sec.

"The poorest are those of 'Marmotte,' at Mortagne—time, 13 min., 26 sec., and of 'Julie,' at Courtalain—time, 11 min. 30 sec.

"Average time of sixty-five trials, 9 min. 15 sec.

"Two and three-fifths miles were made at Illiers by 'Bichette,' in 12 min. 15 sec.

"Two and five-sixths miles were made by same, at same place, and gave an average of 11 min. 30 sec., in three successive heats.

"Three and two-fifths miles were made by 'Champion,' at Illiers, in 12 min.

"HORSES TO HARNESS—TWO MILES—EIGHT RESULTS.

"The best two are those of 'Achille,' at Illiers—time, 7 min. 17 sec., and 'Julie,' same place—time, 7 min. 40½ sec.

"The poorest two are those of 'Championette,' at Illiers—time 7 min. 53 sec., and 'Bichette,' same place—time, 8 min. 13 sec.

"The average of eight trials is about 7 min. 36 sec.

"TWO AND A HALF MILES—FOURTEEN RESULTS.

"The best two are those of 'Vigoreux,' at Illiers—time, 8 min. 30 sec., and 'Bibe,' at Mortagne—time, 9 min. 54 sec.

"The poorest two are those of 'Bichette,' at Courtalain, in 11 min. 30 sec., and of 'Artagan,' at Mortagne, in 11 min. 55 sec.

"TWO AND THREE-FIFTHS MILES—LOADED.

"Two trials were made at Rouen, by 'Decide,' the first drawing 386 pounds in 9 min. 21 sec., the second time drawing 408 pounds in 10 min. 49 sec.

"TRIALS OF ENDURANCE AND SPEED.

"A gray mare, bred by M. Boulavois, at Almeneches (Orne), and belonging to M. Montreauil, horse dealer at Alencon, performed the following match: Harnessed to a traveling-tilbury, she started from Bernay to go to Alencon, a distance of fifty-five and three-fifths miles, over a hilly and difficult road, reaching there in 4 hours and 24 min. This mare is still living, and now belongs to M. Biuson, hotel-keeper at Lees (Orne), where she still draws the omnibus plying between the hotel and station.

"A gray mare seven years old, belonging to M. Cousturur, at Fleury sur Andelle (Eure), harnessed to a tilbury, traveled fifty-eight miles and back on two consecutive days, going at a trot and without being touched with a whip. This was over the road from Lyons la Fossette to Point Andmere and back, through a hilly country. The following time was made: The first day the distance was trotted in 4 hours 1 min. 35 sec., the second day, 4 hours, 1 min. 30 sec. The last thirteen and three-fourths miles were made in one hour, although the mare was obliged to pass her stable at the forty-first mile to finish the distance."

The foregoing history of the Percheron race will give the reader an idea of the origin, development and status of the breed as it exists in France. Although recognized there as the superior of all other draft breeds in that country, the preservation of its pedigrees and the publication of a stud book will add greatly to its value.

DOCILE 5310 (183).

THE PAST AND PRESENT SYSTEM OF BREEDING IN THE PERCHE.

The following extract, quoted from the writings of M. Fardouet, one of the oldest and most prominent breeders of the Perche, and which is fully corroborated by a careful perusal of history, confines its modifications to meet the present developments of the changed condition of the country to three periods of existence.

First—To horses suitable for the saddle and for war.

Second—For agricultural and commercial interests.

Third—The period when the heavy draft-horse, with the activity of the lighter types, came into active demand, which began about fifty years ago. He says:

"This matchless breed, whose antiquity of origin stands first among those of the equine races of civilized nations, has been molded to meet the necessities of the different periods of its existence, for hundreds of years under the vivifying influences and climatic effects of the Perche, as well as by the inimitable processes of educating both males and females from the earliest age, and with the most judicious care possible, by the actual performance of the work they will be called upon to do during their lives, thus slowly and surely developing their physical capabilities and instinctive aptitudes into hereditary and transmissible forces, which have been exerted with such potent power in the amelioration of all races with which it has come in contact.

"In feudal ages the country required a class of horses suited to an equestrian race, *and the Perche supplied them.* With the advent of a higher civilization, the peaceful pursuits of agriculture and commerce demanded horses for the post, the diligence, and for agricultural and draft purposes. *The Perche was called upon, and she met the demand.*

"The application of steam as a motive power introduced a new era in the world's history; the building of railroads and steamships, and its adoption as a power in all the useful arts in manufacturing, has changed all.

"The post and diligence are gone; the agricultural and great commercial marts remain to be supplied; labor and food have become more costly, and the people, by force of necessity and the demands of economy, call for larger, stronger and equally active horses to fill the requirements of the time. How has the Perche sustained herself under the pressure of this last and most difficult demand? The answer fills us with pride and gratification. The government and all the departments of France are eager purchasers of Percheron stallions to improve and ameliorate their native breeds. Russia, Austria, Germany and Italy buy largely, both by direct government purchase and by private enterprise. Even Great Britain, bound up as she is in her own egotism, is a customer of no small magnitude.

"With such magnificent acknowledgments of the value and superiority of the Percheron race we ought to be content, but this is not the half; the plains of South America are being supplied with stock of our breeding, and lastly, that beautiful country, that great republic across the sea, whose progress is the wonder of the world, is our most enamored admirer and liberal purchaser.

"Investigation has shown us that the improvements of the past necessary to meet the changing demands have been accomplished by selecting animals best suited to the new requirements, and by a judicious system of in-and-in-breeding, perpetuating the valuable qualities sought for, at the same time intensifying their hereditary powers of transmitting those qualities; also, that the finest specimens of the Percheron race now in existence are traceable directly to the regenerative influences of the Arab, the primitive horse—the primal origin of the Percheron race.

"The veteran historian and faithful friend of the Percheron, Charles Du Hays, many years ago advocated these doctrines, and it is certainly a most extraordinary commentary upon the discernment and knowledge of horse-breeding possessed by this famous author, that 'Jean le Blanc,' the horse that so greatly excited his admiration that he took the pains to trace his origin, and found him a direct descendant of the famous Arab stallion 'Gallipoli,' belonging to the stud stables of Pin, near Bellesme, established by the Marquis of Brigges in the year 1760, has proven the most potent element in the improvement of the Percheron race, nearly all of the most valuable and highest priced stallions of the Perche being directly traceable to this horse, many of the finest through several lines of in-breeding."

It will thus be seen that the finest and most valuable Percherons—in which is preserved the style, quality and finish of the original type, with the increased weight now demanded, can only be found in individuals descended from animals of Arab origin, increased in size by selecting the largest males and females and a judicious system of in-breeding.

This has resulted in a close relationship of all the finest Percheron families of the present time which are owned by the most progressive and successful breeders and stallioners in the Perche, and *only* in whose possession the finest individuals can be found, in which the same blood is traceable for ages.

The valuable qualities possessed by these animals, that have been concentrated for generations through a careful system of in-and-in-breeding, is the great source of reliance upon which we depend for their prepotency, or the capability of transmitting with absolute certainty the valuable qualities of their race—a power never possessed by animals of mixed blood.

PEGASE 5347 (668).

FAMOUS PERCHERON SIRES.

COCO II (714).

[Recorded with pedigree in the Percheron Stud-Book of France.]

Dapple grey; foaled 1857; bred in the department of the Orne. Got by Vieux Chaslin (713), (belonging to M. Theodore Vinault, of La Ferté-Bernard, department of the Sarthe), he by Coco (712), (belonging to Mr. Chounard; then residing at Champeau, department of Eure-et-Loir), he by Mignon (715), (belonging to M. Poilpre, of Montmirail, Sarthe), he by Jean-le-Blanc (739), a direct descendant of the famous Arab stallion Gallipoli, that stood at the government stud stables at Pin, near Bellesme, about 1820. Coco II. was purchased when a colt by M. Vinault, of La Ferté-Bernard, who kept him until his death. This stallion attained greater fame than any other horse bred in the Perche, not only through his noble ancestry, but from his great individual merit as a stock getter. His grandsire Coco (712) was bred by M. Poilpre, of Montmirail, Sarthe, who sold him, when a suckling colt, to M. Chouanard, who bred from him the famous stallion Vieux Chaslin (713). The dam of Coco (712) was Jeannette by Vieux Coco, belonging to M. Poilpre. The dam of Mignon (715) was a large dapple grey Percheron mare belonging to M. Poilpre.

DÉCIDE (892).

[Recorded with pedigree in the Percheron Stud-Book of France].

Dapple grey; foaled 1856; bred by M. Pelleray of St. Agnan-sur-Sarthe, department of Orne; got by Vieux Pierre (894), (belonging to M. Theodore Vinault, of La Ferté-Bernard), he by Coco (712), he by Mignon (715), he by Jean-le-Blanc (739), etc.; dam Pelote, belonging to M. Berjeau, of Courvalin, Orne; 2d dam Pauline, also belonging to M. Berjeau.

Prosper (893), son of Décidé and sire of Vaillant (404), was also owned by M. Pelleray, his dam being Bourreau by Vieux Pierre (883), belonging to M. Therin of Massuette, department of Orne.

FAVORI I (711).

[Recorded with pedigree in the Percheron Stud-Book of France.]

Foaled 1862; bred near Nogent-le-Rotrou; got by Vieux Chaslin (713), belonging to M. Theodore Vinault, of La Ferté-Bernard, department of the Sarthe), he by Coco (712), (belonging to M. Chounard, then residing at Champeau, department of the Eure-et-Loir), he by Mignon (715), (belonging to M. Poilpre, of Montmirail, Sarthe), he by Jean-le-Blanc (739), (belonging to M. Miard, of Villiers in Ouche (near Sap), department of the Orne, he being a direct descendant of the famous Arab stallion Gallipoli, etc. The dam of Favori I. was Robine, a pure-bred Percheron mare, sired by one of the best Percheron horses of his day, belonging to M. Perriot, the elder, then residing at Amilly, department of the Orne.

Favori I. was owned by M. Perriot, the elder, and was one of the famous horses of the Perche, and, as will be seen by this catalogue, many lines of breeding trace directly to him.

ILDERIM (5302).

[Recorded with pedigree in the Percheron Stud-Book of France.]

Grey; foaled 1859; bred by M. Haye, of Vilousier, near Châteaudun, department of Eure-et-Loir; got by Valentin (530), (belonging to M. Theodore Vinault, of La Ferté-Bernard), he by Vieux Chaslin (713), etc.; dam Chaton (belonging to M. Haye), by Vieux Pierre (894), (belonging to M, Vinault), he by Coco (712), etc. Ilderim was sold at the age of five months to M. Ravaut, of Vilousier, and by him sold to the Société Hippique of Eure-et-Loir, who stood him several years. It was during his "courses" for that Society that he sired the famous horse French Monarch 205 (734), the figures in the pedigrees of many of the best horses imported to this country.

LUTHER (792).

[Recorded with pedigree in the Percheron Stud-Book of France.

Bay; foaled May 16, 1869; bred and owned by M. Anatole Miard, of Echauffer, department of the Orne. Got by Pierre (887), (belonging to M. Miard), he by Laboureur (886), (also belonging to M. Miard), he by Jean-le-Blanc (739), (belonging to M. Miard the elder), he being a direct descendant of the famous Arab stallion Gallipoli, etc.; dam Rosette belonging to M. Miard and sired by Laboureur (886). The dam of Pierre was Margot by Faisan. The dam of Laboureur was Sophie by Sandi. In the Perche the name of this family of horses and the name of Miard are synonymous terms, as for over half a century this strain has been bred in all its purity by the Miards, father and son, until to-day it stands preëminently forth as one of the grandest families of the Percheron race.

JUPITER AT ISLAND HOME.

Jupiter, the subject of the rare and treasured sketch from which the engraving on the opposite page was made, deserves more than passing notice, and likewise the engraving. Early in 1884, to increase the popularity of French horses in America, the Percheron Society of France, under authority of the French government, selected six Percheron stallions, the finest of the race, one of them being Jupiter 3692 (216), and appealed to the boundless generosity and unwavering patriotism of the renowned Rosa Bonheur, the most celebrated animal painter the world has ever known, to sketch them.

Rosa Bonheur, never found wanting in national pride and enterprise, and to lend added lustre to the fame of her beloved Percherons, immortalized a score of years since in her celebrated painting, "Going to the Fair," undertook the task. The stallions were taken to her chateau and there retained until the sketches were completed. Jupiter was imported in November, 1884, and to-day Island Home stud is graced with his royal presence. As a further evidence of the great superiority of this horse, he being Rosa Bonheur's choice of the six (and she is acknowledged by all breeders of Percheron horses to be the best judge of them), she completed a large oil painting of Jupiter, and it was on exhibition in Paris during the last summer.

He has a lofty carriage, most elegantly rounded body, unequaled back, quarters and flank, three points seldom ever found in one animal, all in a high order of perfection. He stands squarely and perfectly upon his legs, which are very clean and free from hair; his feet are the very best, his action high, easy and graceful. (For pedigree see page 36.)

JUPITER 3692 (216)

ISLAND HOME.

PLUVIOSE 3755 (683).

[Recorded with pedigree in the Percheron Stud-Books of France and America.]

Dark grey; 16¼ hands; weight 1,810 lbs.; foaled February, 1882; imported 1884; bred by M. Goupil, of La Roussetiere, commune of Souance, canton of Nogent-Le-Rotrou, department of Eure-et-Loir; got by Narbonne 1334 (777), he by Brilliant 1899 (756), he by Coco II. (714) (for extension of pedigree see page 27); dam Paquerette by Superior 454 (730), he by Favori I. (711) (for extension of pedigree see page 27). At the great Percheron Show held at Chicago, September, 1886, Pluviose was the winner of second prize in a ring pronounced the best lot of draft four-year-olds ever brought together. A compact yet stylish and very active horse, full of vigor and energy. In general form his harmony of proportion is rarely equaled, being unusually good in almost every point, is an extra good walker, and trots at a very rapid gait for such a heavy horse. (For cut see page 9.)

JUPITER 3692 (216).

[Recorded with pedigree in the Percheron Stud-Books of France and America.]

Grey; 16¼ hands; weight 1,810 lbs.; foaled February, 1881; imported 1884; bred by M. Jousset, of La Saussie, commune of St. Aubin-d'Appenai, canton of Mesle-sur-Sarthe, department of Orne; got by Voltaire (belonging to M. Felix Gasselin, of La Bretonniere, commune of Laleux, canton of Mesle-sur-Sarthe, department of Orne), he by Monarque, (also owned by M. Gasselin), he by Coco II. (714) (for extension of pedigree see page 27); dam L'Amie (6008) by Romulus 873 (785), he by the Government approved stallion Romulus, he by the Government approved stallion Moreuil. This colt has a lofty carriage, most elegantly rounded body, unequaled back, quarters and flank, three points seldom ever found in one animal, all in a high order of perfection. He stands squarely and perfectly upon his legs, which are very clean and free from hair; his feet are the very best, his action high, easy and graceful. He was a prize winner at the great Percheron show held at Chicago in September, 1886. (For cut see page 29.)

ROMULUS 873 (785).

[Recorded with pedigree in the Percheron Stud Books of France and America.]

Dapple grey; 16¼ hands; weight 1,875 lbs.; foaled 1873; imported 1879; bred by M. Caget; got by the Government approved stallion Romulus (belonging to M. Caget); he by Moreuil, a stallion approved by the Government (also belonging to M. Caget); dam Fleur d'Epine by the Government approved stallion Cheri, he by the Government approved stallion Carbon. Romulus is therefore bred from two famous horses, both winners of *First Prizes* at all the great Concours of France during their time; who thus transmitted to their son and grandson the qualities that won for him the *First Prize* and Gold Medal at the *Universal Exposition* of Paris in 1878. Also, First Prize and Gold Medal at the Grand Concours of Evereux, 1879; and Thirty other first Prizes in 1878, two for trotting. He is a very fast walker, which is a most valuable characteristic of the Percheron horse; has fine action, and is a wonderful trotter for so heavy a horse. For stock he was unsurpassed by any draft or all purpose horse in France. No description could be given of this horse that would do him justice: the fact that the highest honors were conferred upon him at the Universal Exhibition of Paris, 1878, the greatest show the World has ever known, will give an idea of his matchless qualities. The exultant shouts of "Vive le Percheron!" "Vive le Percheron!" of thousands in the Amphitheatre as Romulus, at the head of all the horses on exhibition from every part of Europe, WAS LED PAST THE TRIBUNE, occupied by the President of the French Republic, and all the official dignitaries of the nation, speaks plainer than any words can of this famous horse. (For cut see page 33.)

IMPORTED AND PURE BRED STALLIONS.

ATHIS 5282 (6771).

[Recorded with pedigree in the Percheron Stud Books of France and America.]

Black; 16 hands high; weight 1,620 lbs.; foaled May 1, 1884; imported 1886; bred by M. Joseph Bouet, of La Basse-Cour, commune of Souge-le-Ganelon, department of Sarthe; got by Parisien (2509), he by Parisien, he by Favori (belonging to M. Croize); dam Castille (7660) (belonging to M. Joseph Bouet). This colt has a bright intelligent face and slightly Roman nose, indicating the courage and energy he possesses; well crested neck, sloping shoulder, long round body, with heavy arm and stifle development, wide hock, and stands squarely on his feet, which are, like Percherons generally, of the best. Athis won first prize at the Michigan State Fair, held at Jackson in September, 1886.

BISMARK 5747.

Dark bay; foaled Oct. 11, 1886; bred at Island Home; got by Brilliant 3867 (2706), he by Bayard, he by Thomas; dam Nini 3883 (2688) by Passe Partout (1402), he by Comet 104 (719), he by French Monarch 205 (734), he by Ilderim (5302) (for extension of pedigree see page 27).

BLOND'OR 5281 (7350).

[Recorded with pedigree in the Percheron Stud Books of France and America.]

Grey; 16 hands; weight, 1650 lbs.; foaled May 28, 1883; imported 1886; bred by M. Moreau, of Terte, commune of Courgenard, department of Sarthe; got by Clement 1965 (936), he by Philibert (760), he by Superior 454 (730), he by Favori I. (711) (for extension of pedigree see page 27; dam Rose (7349) by Coco II. (714), (for extension of pedigree see page 27).

BUFFON 2389 (1098).

[Recorded with pedigree in the Percheron Stud Books of France and America.]

Black; 16 hands high; weight 1,800 lbs.; foaled 1880; imported by M. Felix Gasselin, of Mesle-sur-Sarthe, department of Orne; got by Brilliant 1271 (755), he by Brilliant 1899 (756), he by Coco II. (714) (for extension of pedigree see page 27); dam L'Amie by Superior 454(730), he by Favori I. (711) (for extension of pedigree see page 27). In color, form and action an exact prototype of his sire, the celebrated Brilliant. (For cut see page 33.)

CESAR III. 5278 (5058).

[Recorded with pedigree in the Percheron Stud Books of France and America.]

Black grey; 16½ hands high; weight 1,650 lbs.; foaled March 18, 1883; imported 1886; bred by M. Lebreton, of Ravallier, commune of La Perriere, canton of Pervencheres, department of Orne; got by Vidocq (belonging to M. Jousset, pere); he by Brilliant (also owned by M. Jousset); dam Brilliante (5059) by Selim (749), he by Porthos. This colt has a small head, prominent bright eyes, well crested neck, heavy arm and stifle, short back, full loin, long level quarter, wide flat legs, with good and spirited action.

CHAMPAIGN 3678.

[Recorded with pedigree in the Percheron Stud Book of America.]

Blue grey; 16 hands; weight 1,620 lbs.; foaled 1882; got by Black Prince 1574; dam La Belle 974. Head carried high, deep shoulders, broad in breast and stifles, well rounded body, heavy and clean limbs, remarkable feet, and a colt giving promise of becoming an excellent breeder.

ROMULUS 873 (795).

CHANDON 2620 (32).

[Recorded with pedigree in the Percheron Stud Books of France and America.]

Bright bay; 16¼ hands; weight 1,750 lbs.; foaled 1882; imported 1883; bred by M. Magloire Poulain, of St. Aubin-d'Appenay, canton of Mesle-sur-Sarthe, department of Orne; got by Voltaire (5728), he by Coco, of the Mesle-sur-Sarthe, he by Margot; dam Cocotte by Romulus 873 (785), he by the Government approved stallion Romulus (belonging to M. Celestin Caget, of Almeneches, department of Orne), he by the Government approved stallion Moreuil, also owned by M. Celestin Caget. He has a bright clean face with a star, large prominent eyes, well crested neck, lofty carriage, full black points, a heavy mane and tail, clean limbs, and a remarkably stylish horse throughout.

CHERI 5270 (7348).

[Recorded with pedigree in the Percheron Stud Books of France and America.]

Grey; 15¼ hands; weight 1,790 lbs.; foaled April 5, 1883; imported 1886; bred by M. Modeste Deshayes, of La Fosse, commune of Boccé, canton of Bazoches-sur-Hoene, department of Orne; got by Bon Cœur (7346), he by Bon Cœur (belonging to the French Government); dam Margot (7347) by Coco (belonging to M. L. Vallee, of Condé, commune of La Mencire, canton of Bazoches-sur-Hoene, department of Orne). Cheri has a clean, smooth and straight head, neck well set on his body, short back, good loin and long level hip, very heavy bone, good action, and destined to make a large, powerful horse. He has been approved by the French Government.

CLOTAIRE 5345 (6232).

[Recorded with pedigree in the Percheron Stud Books of France and America.]

Dapple grey; 16¼ hands; weight 1,820 lbs.; foaled April 15, 1883; imported 1886; bred by M. Sagot, of Pré, commune of Chapelle Guillaume, canton of Authon, department of Eure-et-Loir; got by Colin (5723), he by Colin (belonging to M. Lucas, of Montmirail, department of Sarthe); dam Bijou (6231), by La Douceur (belonging to M. Bataille, of Souday, department of Loir-et-Cher). Clotaire has a clean straight face, ears well set, small muzzle and well crested neck, deep full chest, heavy muscled arm and stifle, high withers, short back, full loin and level quarter, with heavy bone, and a remarkably easy and fast mover for so heavy a horse. He was a prize winner at the Great Percheron Concours, held at Nogent Le Rotrou, France, June, 1886.

CLOVIS 5346 (6234).

[Recorded with pedigree in the Percheron Stud Books of France and America.]

Dark grey; 16¼ hands, weight 1,830 lbs.; foaled March 10, 1883; bred by M. Sagot, of Pré, commune of Chapelle Guillaume, canton of Authon, department of Eure-et-Loir; got by Colin (5723), he by Colin (belonging to M. Lucas, of Montmirail, department of Sarthe); dam Margot (6233), by La Douceur (belonging to M. Bataille, of Souday, department of Loir-et-Cher). Clovis has a clean well shaped head, long well crested neck, high withers and deep chest, very clean symmetrical legs, deep flank and well ribbed down, high, full loin, long quarter, well muscled on the stifle, and remarkably stylish for so heavy a horse. He was a prize winner at the Great National Concourse, held at Nogent Le Rotrou, France, in June, 1886. (For cut see page 18.)

DECIDE 5574 (1666).

[Recorded with pedigree in the Percheron Stud Books of France and America.]

Dapple grey; 15¼ hands, weight 1,650 lbs.; imported 1886; bred by M. Briere, of La Haye, commune of La-Chapelle-Souef, canton of Belleme, department of Orne; got by Madere (2994), he by Madeira 1546 (770), he by Vidocq 483 (732), he by Coco II. (714) (for extension of pedigree see page 27); dam L'Amie (4614) by Madeira 1546 (770), etc.; 2d dam Bicotte by Bayard. Decide has a clean medium sized head, rather short but well crested neck, heavily muscled arm, long round body, broad quarter and stifle, with spirited and lofty carriage.

DOCILE 5310 (183).

[Recorded with pedigree in the Percheron Stud Books of France and America.]

Black, with star in forehead; 16¼ hands; weight 1,750 lbs; foaled 1882; imported 1886; bred by M Nion, commune of Coudray-au-Perche, canton of Authon, department of Eure-et Loir; got by Vaillant (6752), he by Bayard (6751), he by Mina (belonging to the Societe Hippique Eure-et-Loir); dam La Poule (7468) by Vieux Vaillant (1388), he by Pierre, belonging to M Therin. Docile has a short head broad between the eyes, very broad chest, long round body and well ribbed down, good clean legs and stands squarely on them, good action, and a very spirited and pleasant disposition. He was a prize winner at the Great Concours, held at Nogent Le Rotrou, France, June, 1886. (For cut see page 22.)

GRISON 5274 (5700).

[Recorded with pedigree in the Percheron Stud Books of France and America.]

Dark grey; 16¼ hands; weight 1,630 lbs.; foaled May 4, 1883; imported 1886; bred by M. Metais, of La Cholire, commune of Ruille-sur-Loir, canton of Chartres, department of Eure et Loir; got by Coco (4796), he by Paul (belonging to M. Dubois, of Ruille-sur-Loir); dam Cocotte (5699) by Charlot (belonging to M. Mauclair, of Ruille-sur-Loir). A very intelligent, bright colt, with a clean, fine head; is smooth and uniform throughout, and a very fast stepper.

HECTOR 5707.

[Recorded with pedigree in the Percheron Stud Book of America.]

Black; foaled August 5, 1886; bred at Island Home; got by Pluviose 3755 (683), he by Narbonne 1334 (777), he by Brilliant 1899 (756), he by Coco II. (714) for extension of pedigree see page 27); dam Pelotte 3866 (2622) by Lamoureux, he by Favora 1542 (765), he by French Monarch 205 (734), he by Ilderim (5302) (for extension of pedigree see page 27); 2d dam Rosette by Solide. A fine colt, and all that his breeding indicates.

JENA 5279 (483).

[Recorded with pedigree in the Percheron Stud Books of France and America.]

Black; 17 hands; weight 1,890 lbs.; foaled 1883; imported 1886; bred by M. Chatton, of Plessis, commune of Ceton, canton of Theil, department of Orne; got by Vidocq (1403), he by Utopia 780 (731), he by Superior 454 (730), he by Favori I. (711) (for extension of pedigree see page 27); dam Sophie (7454) by Iago 995 (768), he by Utopia 780 (731), etc. This colt has a clean bony head, deep chest, well ribbed down, heavy bone, fair action for so drafty a horse.

JUPITER 3692 (216).

[Recorded with pedigree in the Percheron Stud Books of France and America.]

Grey; 16½ hands; weight 1,810 lbs ; foaled February. 1881; imported 1884; bred by M. Jousset, of La Saussie, commune of St. Aubin-d'Appenai, canton of Mesle-sur Sarthe, department of Orne; got by Voltaire (belonging to M. Felix Gasselin, of La Bretonniere, commune of Laleux,. canton of Mesle sur-Sarthe. department of Orne), he by Monarque (also owned by M. Gasselin), he by Coco II. (714) (for extension of pedigree see page 27); dam L'Amie (6008) by Romulus 873 (785), he by the Government approved stallion Romulus, he by the Government approved stallion Moreuil. This colt has a lofty carriage, most elegantly rounded body, unequalled back, quarters and flank, three points seldom ever found in one animal, all in a high order of perfection. He stands squarely and perfectly upon his legs, which are very clean and free from hair; his feet are the very best, his action, high, easy and graceful. He was a prize winner at the great Percheron show held at Chicago in September, 1886. (For cut see page 29.)

LA MARQUE 2883.

[Recorded in the Percheron Stud Book of America.]

Black; 16½ hands; weight 1,640 lbs.; foaled 1879; imported 1882. A smooth, compact horse, with fair action, and a good breeder.

LAMBRA 3653 (117).

[Recorded with pedigree in the Percheron Stud Books of France and America.]

Dark grey; 16¼ hands; weight 1,890 lbs.; foaled March 21, 1883; imported 1884; bred by M. Noireau, of La Diabliere, commune of Ceton, canton of Theil, department of Orne; got by Taconet 2581 (1307), he by Brilliant (710), he by Brilliant 1899 (756), he by Coco II. (714) (for extension of pedigree see page 27); dam Bleue,.by Favori I. (711) (for extension of pedigree see page 27). Lambra has a clean, rather short, bony head, wide between the eyes. clean throttle and a well crested neck, deep chest, full black points, very clean limbs free from hair, and is a good mover.

LE PETIT DUC 4167.

[Recorded with pedigree in the Percheron Stud Book of America.]

Silver grey; 15¼ hands; weight 1,360 lbs.; foaled 1884; got by Romulus 873 (785), he by the Government approved stallion Romulus, he by the Government approved stallion Moreuil; dam Cozette 884 by Selim (749), he by Porthos. Le Petit Duc is as perfect as a picture in every point, resembling greatly his noted sire Romulus, who took first prize at the Paris Exposition in 1878.

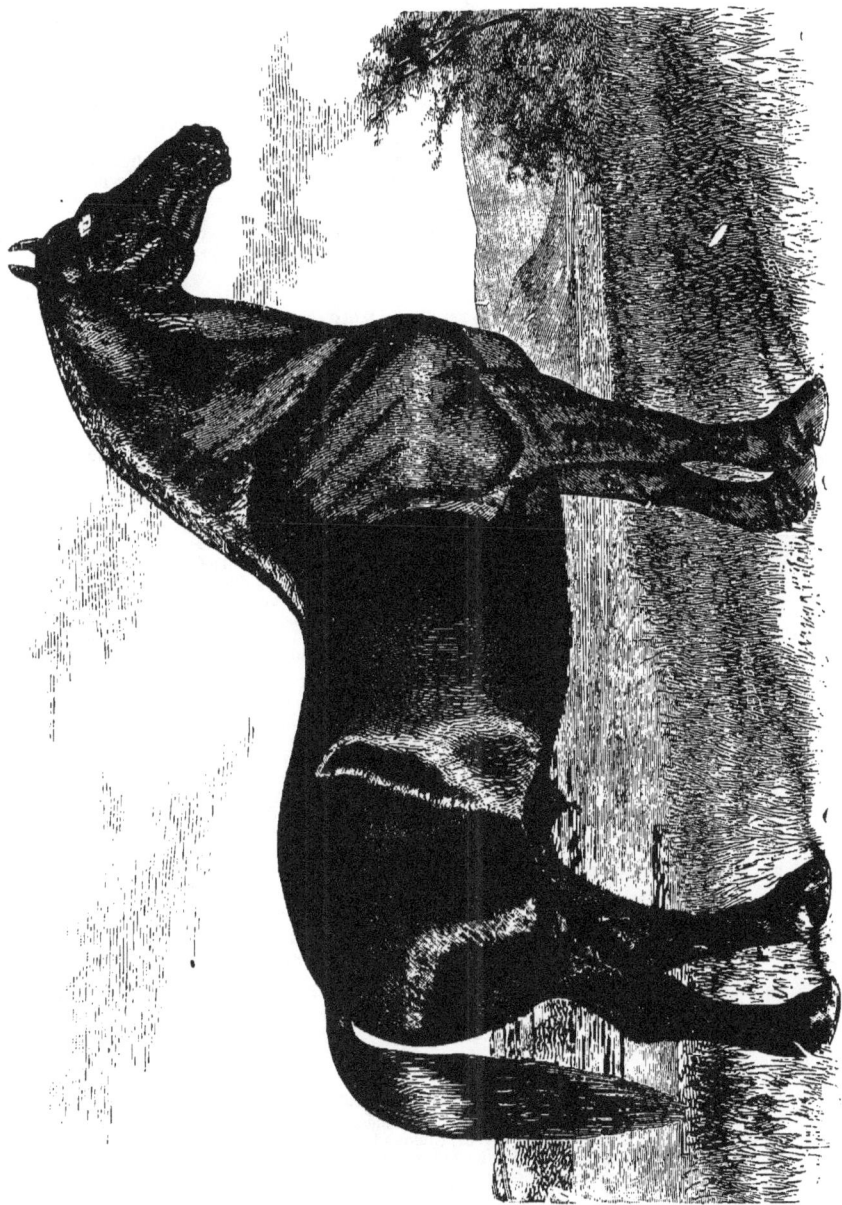

BUFFON 2389 (1098).

LORENDO 4991 (5036).

[Recorded with pedigree in the Percheron Stud Books of France and America.]

Grey; 16¼ hands; weight 1,730 lbs.; foaled May 25, 1884; bred by M. Miteau, of Genettes, commune of Essai, canton of Mesle-sur-Sarth, department of Orne; got by Genator (2613), he by Favora 1542 (765), he by French Monarch 205 (734), he by Ilderim (5002) (for extension of pedigree see page 27); dam Poule (1892) by Solide (belonging to M. Miteau), he by the Government approved stallion Margot. He has a short, clean head, and is broad between the eyes, deep chest, and a long, deep body, good loin, and a remarkably level quarter, very straight, clean flat legs, and excellent feet, upon which he stands squarely, and has a smooth, straight action. Lorendo was a prize winner at the great Percheron Show, held at Chicago, in September, 1886, and at Michigan State Fair, held at Jackson same month.

MARIOTTI 5271 (5630).

[Recorded with pedigree in the Percheron Stud Books of France and America.]

Grey; 16¼ hands; weight 1860 lbs.; foaled April 30, 1884; imported 1886; bred by Madame Grison, of Marolles-les-Braux, canton of Marolles-les-Braux, department of Sarthe; got by Abdel Kader (5609), he by Favori (belonging to M. Lefeuvre, of Mercorbon, commune of Marolles-les-Braux); dam Charmante (5629) by Coco (belonging to M. Lefeuvre). Mariotti has a clean straight face, long well crested neck, deep chest, good loin and quarter, clean well formed legs, on which he stands squarely, and he is destined to make a very large, fine horse.

NOIRAUD 5268 (5626).

[Recorded with pedigree in the Percheron Stud Books of France and America.]

Black, no white; 16¼ hands; weight 1,740 lbs.; foaled April 30, 1884; imported 1886; bred by M. Odillard, of Avesnes, canton of Marolles-les-Braux, department of Sarthe; got by Vermouth (5608), he by Picador I. (belonging to M. Lefeuvre, of Le Meniere, canton of Bazoche-sur-Hoene, department of Orne); dam Moustache (5625) by Bayard I. (belonging to F. Lefeuvre). Noiraud has a clean, bony head, small ears, well set, finely crested neck well set on his body, high withers, full loin and quarter, clean well shaped legs free from hair, with good action.

ORIENTAL 4210 (223).

[Recorded with pedigree in the Percheron Stud Books of France and America.]

Dapple grey; 17 hands; weight 2,000 lbs.; foaled March 16, 1880; imported 1885; bred by M. Rottior, of Chatelier, commune of Cherre, canton of La-Ferte-Bernard, department of Sarthe; got by Favori (1401), he by Favora 1542 (765), he by French Monarch 205 (734), he by Ilderim (5302) (for extension of pedigree see page 27); dam Bijou (4908) by Favora 1542 (765), etc. Oriental has prominent eyes, fine ears, beautiful head, well crested neck, deep chest, and body well ribbed down, good quarter, clean legs, and is a very smooth and stylish horse for so large a one.

PASSE PARTOUT 4165.

[Recorded with pedigree in the Percheron Stud Book of America.]

Black grey; 17 hands; weight 1,740 lbs.; foaled 1884; got by Romulus 873 (785), he by the Government approved stallion Romulus, he by the Government approved stallion Mereuil; dam Fantine 887 by Brilliant 1899 (756), he by Coco II. (714) (for extension of pedigree see page 27). Passe Partout is clean, smooth and symmetrical throughout, like all the stock of his sire, the celebrated Romulus.

PAUL 5704 (187).

[Recorded with pedigree in the Percheron Stud Books of France and America.]

Dark bay; 16¼ hands; weight 1,860 lbs; foaled January 1, 1883; imported 1886; bred by M. Nion, of Coudray-au-Perche, canton of Authon, department of Eure-et-Loir; got by Madere (5308), he by Mouton (1640), he by French Monarch 205 (734), he by Ilderim (5302) (for extension of pedigree see page 27); dam Chaton (7469) by Colin (belonging to M. Sagot), he by Bayard (6751), he by Mina (belonging to the Societe Hippique Eure-et-Loir). Paul has a rather large, bony head, prominent eye, heavy mane and tail, deep chest, flank well let down, long quarter, heavy boned, and is a good mover.

PEGASE 5347 (668).

[Recorded with pedigree in the Percheron Stud Books of France and America.]

Dark dapple grey; 16 hands; weight 1,730 lbs.; foaled April 7, 1883; imported 1886; bred by M. Dieu, of Colombier, commune of Souance, canton of Nogent-le-Rotrou, department of Eure-et-Loir; got by Vaillant (404), he by Prosper (893), he by Decide (892) (for extension of pedigree see page 27); dam L'Amie (7301) by Madere (belonging to M. Louis Perriot, of Champeaux, near Nogent-le-Rotrou). He has a clean, medium-sized head, well set on a finely crested neck, good loin, and a remarkably long, level quarter, well ribbed down in the flank. clean nervy limbs and the best of feet, and is a smooth and spirited mover. Pegase won first prize at the Michigan State Fair, held at Jackson in September, 1886. (For cut see page 26.)

PLANET 911 (811).

[Recorded with pedigree in the Percheron Stud Books of France and America.]

Dapple grey; 16¼ hands; weight 1,710 lbs.; foaled 1880; imported 1880; got by Philibert (760), he by Superior 454 (730), he by Favori (711) (for extension of pedigree see page 27). This horse has a very long and full white mane and tail, and is very smooth and clean in his outlines, with a very stylish and coachy appearance.

PLUVIOSE 3755 (683).

[Recorded with pedigree in the Percheron Stud Books of France and America.]

Dark grey; 16¼ hands; weight 1,810 lbs.; foaled February, 1882; imported 1884; bred by M. Goupil, of La Roussetiere, commune of Souance, canton of Nogent-Le-Rotrou, department of Eure-et-Loir; got by Narbonne 1334 (777), he by Brilliant 1899 (756), he by Coco II. (714) (for extension of pedigree see page 27); dam Paquerette by Superior 454 (730), he by Favori I. (711) (for extension of pedigree see page 27). At the great Percheron Show held at Chicago, September, 1886, Pluviose was the winner of second prize in a ring pronounced the best lot of draft four-year-olds ever brought together. A compact yet stylish and very active horse, full of vigor and energy. In general form his harmony of proportion is rarely equaled, being unusually good in almost every point, is an extra good walker, and trots at a very rapid gait for such a heavy horse. (For cut see page 9.)

PRIMUS 5705.

[Recorded with pedigree in the Percheron Stud Book of America.]

Black grey; foaled May 26, 1886; bred at Island Home; got by Pluviose 3755 (683), he by Narbonne 1334 (777), he by Brilliant 1899 (756), he by Coco II. (714) (for extension of pedigree see page 27); dam Isis 1744 by Chaldean 637 (854), he by Coco II. (714) (for extension of pedigree see page 27); 2d dam Clara Belle 795.

PRINCEPS 4166.

[Recorded with pedigree in the Percheron Stud Book of America.]

Black grey; 15¼ hands; weight 1,460 lbs; foaled 1884; got by Romulus 873 (785), he by the Government approved stallion Romulus, he by the Government approved stallion Moreuil; dam Juno 891 by Duke de Chartres 162 (721), he by Coco II. (714) (for extension of pedigree see page 27); 2d dam Fleur d'Epine, by the Government approved stallion Cheri, he by the Government approved stallion Corbon. This is a very clean, smooth and symmetrical colt, like all the progeny of his illustrious sire Romulus.

PRINCE VICTOR 5004 (5601).

[Recorded with pedigree in Percheron Stud Books of France and America.]

Dark grey; 16 hands; weight 1,600 lbs.; foaled April 14, 1884; imported 1886; bred by M. Gautier, of Montmirail, France; got by Coco (5701). he by Coco (owned by M. Tacheau, and imported to America in 1880); dam Brebis (5600) by Cheri (owned by M. Gautier, of Montmirail). A very stylish colt with a lofty carriage.

ST. LAURENT 3486 (2671).

RALPH 5269 (661).

[Recorded with pedigree in the Percheron Stud Books of France and America.]

Steel grey; 16¼ hands; weight 1,680 lbs; foaled February, 1883; imported 1886; bred by M. Poussin, of Nogent-le-Rotrou, department of Eure-et-Loir; got by Brilliant (1737), he by L'Ami (1388), he by Coco, he by Coco II. (714) (for extension of pedigree see page 27); dam Bijou (7305) by Marquis (belonging to M. Charles Aveline, commune of Verrieres, canton of Noce, department of Orne) He has a clean bony head finely set on a beautifully crested neck, full loin, level quarter, flank well let down, and very clean limbs, with good action. A particularly smooth and stylish colt. Ralph was the winner of the second prize at the Great Percheron Show, held at Chicago, September, 1886.

ROMULUS 873 (785).

[Recorded with pedigree in the Percheron Stud Books of France and America.]

Dapple grey; 16¼ hands; weight, 1,875 lbs.; foaled 1873; imported 1879; bred by M. Caget; got by the Government approved stallion Romulus (belonging to M. Caget); he by Morcuil, a stallion approved by the Government (also belonging to M. Caget); dam Fleur d'Epine by the Government approved stallion Cheri, he by the Government approved stallion Carbon. Romulus is therefore bred from two famous horses, both winners of *First Prizes* at all the great Concours of France during their time; who thus transmitted to their son and grandson the qualities that won for him the *First Prize* and Gold Medal at the *Universal Exposition* of Paris in 1878. Also, First Prize and Gold Medal at the Grand Concours of Evereux, 1879; and Thirty other first Prizes in 1878, two for trotting. He is a very fast walker, which is a most valuable characteristic of the Percheron horse; has fine action, and is a wonderful trotter for so heavy a horse. For stock he was unsurpassed by any draft or all purpose horse in France. No description could be given of this horse that would do him justice; the fact that the highest honors were conferred upon him at the Universal Exhibition of Paris, 1878, the greatest show the World has ever known, will give an idea of his matchless qualities. The exultant shouts of "Vive le Percheron !" "Vive le Percheron !" of thousands in the Amphitheatre as Romulus, at the head of all the horses on exhibition from every part of Europe, WAS LED PAST THE TRIBUNE, occupied by the President of the French Republic, and all the official dignitaries of the nation, speaks plainer than any words can of this famous horse. (For cut see page 33.)

ROMULUS 3529 (698).

[Recorded with pedigree in the Percheron Stud Books of France and America.]

Dark grey, with star in forehead; 17 hands; weight 1,810 lbs., foaled April 9, 1883; imported 1884; bred by M. Boisseau, of St. Cyr-la-Rosiere, canton of Noce, department of Orne; got by Cheri, he by Count 643 (736), he by Bayard 26 (717), he by Favori I. (711) (for extension of pedigree see page 27); dam Pauline by Luther (792), he by Pierre (887) (for extension of pedigree see page 27). Romulus has a short, bony head, broad between the eyes, rather short but well crested neck, deep chest, good flank, smooth legs free from hair, and a fair mover for a large horse.

RUBENS 5273 (7041).

[Recorded with pedigree in the Percheron Stud Books of France and America.]

Silver grey; 16¼ hands; weight 1,820 lbs.; foaled April 24, 1883; imported 1886; bred by M. Brette, of La Beaucerie, commune of Bethonvilliers, canton of Authon, department of Eure-et-Loir; got by Vaillant (6752), he by Bayard (6751), he by Mina (belonging to the Societe Hippique Eure-et-Loir); dam by Cocote (7040) by Vaillant (6752), etc. Rubens has a medium-sized bony head, clean throttle, deep chest and flank; long quarter, with rather short but clean nervy legs, and good feet. Will make a very blocky horse.

ST. LAURENT 3486 (2671).

[Recorded with pedigree in the Percheron Stud Books of France and America.]

Black, with star on forehead; 16¼ hands; weight 1,670 lbs.; foaled April 18, 1884; imported 1885; bred by M. Lesault, commune of Breval Gatineau, canton of La-Ferte-Bernard, department of Sarthe; got by Docile (446); he by Brilliant 1899 (756); he by Coco II. (714) (for extension of pedigree see page 27); dam Lisa (belonging to M. Lesault) by Favori 666 (725); he by Favori I. (711) (for extension of pedigree see page 27). This is a deep chested heavily built colt, resembling very much his grandsire, Brilliant.

SEBASTOPOL 5272 (7043).

[Recorded with pedigree in the Percheron Stud Books of France and America.]

Silver grey; 16½ hands; weight 1,840 lbs.; foaled March 17, 1883; imported 1886; bred by M. Brette, of La Beaucerie, commune of Bethonvilliers, canton of Authon, department of Eure-et-Loir; got by Vaillant (6752), he by Bayard (6751), he by Mina (belonging to the Societe Hippique Eure-et-Loir); dam Chaton (7042) by Vigoureux (1392), he by Coco II. (714) (for extension of pedigree see page 27). Sebastopol possesses a good medium sized, clean head, clean throttle, deep broad chest, flank well let down, long quarter, short, heavy boned but clean legs. He was a very popular sire in France last season.

SENATOR 5603 (4120).

[Recorded with pedigree in the Percheron Stud Books of France and America.]

Dark dapple grey; 15¾ hands; weight 1,560 lbs.; foaled 1884; imported 1886; bred by M. Manoury, commune of Pervencheres, department of Orne; got by Romulus 3523 (222), he by Prosper (893), he by Decide (892) (for extension of pedigree see page 27); dam Sublette (4119) by Athos, he by Porthos. A clean-made, stylish colt.

SOLFERINO 4155 (2798).

[Recorded with pedigree in the Percheron Stud Books of France and America.]

Grey black; 17 hands high; weight 1,840 lbs.; foaled April 15, 1882; imported 1885; bred by M. Prudent Fleury, commune of Prevencheres, department of Orne; got by Bon Couer (belonging to M. Fardouet, Sr.), he by Bon Couer of Etas; dam Laucette, belonging to M. Fleury, commune of Prevencheres, department of Orne.

TELEMAQUE 5280 (2034).

[Recorded with pedigree in the Percheron Stud Books of France and America.]

Dapple grey; 16¾ hands; weight 1,690 lbs.; foaled 1882; imported 1886; bred by M. Chaillou, of Grand Bure, commune of La Rouge, canton of Theil, department of Orne; got by Vaillant (404), he by Prosper (893), he by Decide (892) (for extension of pedigree see page 27); dam La Pelotte (7540) by Vaillant (1383), he by Pierre (belonging to M. Therin). Telemaque is broad between the eyes, ears well set, long smooth body and hips, heavy boned, and a good mover.

TROILUS 5706.

[Recorded with pedigree in the Percheron Stud Book of America.]

Black grey; foaled June 11, 1886; bred at Island Home; got by Pluviose 3755 (683), he by Narbonne 1331 (777), he by Brilliant 1899 (756), he by Coco II. (714) (for extension of pedigree see page 27); dam Elise 3869 (2618) by Vermouth; 2d dam Mignonne by Solide.

VAILLANT 5569 (189).

[Recorded with pedigree in the Percheron Stud Books of France and America.]

Dark grey; 17 hands; weight 1,890 lbs.; foaled January, 1883; imported 1886; bred by M. Charron, of La Grofardiere, commune of St. Hilaire-sur-Erre, canton of Theil, department of Orne; got by Vaillant (404), he by Prosper (893), he by Decide (892) (for extension of pedigree see page 27); dam Pelotte (4497) by Papillon (belonging to M. Therin, of Massuette). Vaillant has a rather large bony head, long round body, extraordinarily large arm and stifle, with uncommonly heavy bone and joints.

VICTOR 4164.

[Recorded with pedigree in the Percheron Stud Book of America.]

Dark grey; 15¼ hands; weight 1,500 lbs.; foaled 1883; got by Romulus 873 (785), he by the Government approved stallion Romulus, he by the Government approved stallion Moreuil; dam Cozette 884 by Selim (749), he by Porthos. A very smooth, clean and stylish colt; in fact, perfection in every point.

VIGILANT 5275 (6238).

[Recorded with pedigree in the Percheron Stud Books of France and America.]

Dapple grey; 16¾ hands; weight 1,880 lbs; foaled May 1, 1883; imported 1886; bred by M. Gaultier, of La Reine Boudiere, commune of Lamnay, canton of Montmirail, department of Sarthe; got by Decide (belonging to M. Vinault of La-Ferte Bernard), he by Favori I. (711) (for extension of pedigree see page 27); dam Pimpante (6237) by Favori (belonging to M. Vinault). Vigilante possesses a clean straight head, well set small ears, remarkably long, well set and crested neck, high withers, long round body, long quarters, heavy arm and stifle, heavy boned, clean, nervy legs, making a remarkably stylish horse, with the best of action.

VLADIMIR 5276 (2996).

[Recorded with pedigree in the Percheron Stud Books of France and America.]

Black; 16¼ hands; weight 1,600 lbs.; foaled April 28, 1883; imported 1886; bred by M. Desire Ducoeurjoly, of La Fontaine, commune of Brunelles, canton of Nogent-le-Rotrou, department of Eure-et-Loir; got by Bienfaisant (1397), he by Vermouth 1820 (787), he by Vidocq 483 (732), he by Coco II. (714) (for extension of pedigree see page 27); dam Grisette (280) by Medoc I., he by French Monarch 205 (734), he by Ilderim (5302) (for extension of pedigree see page 27); 2d dam Pauline (279) by Miramar. Vladimir is smooth, uniform and compactly built, with good action.

VOLTAIRE 5703 (186).

[Recorded with pedigree in the Percheron Stud Books of France and America.]

Brown bay; 16¼ hands; weight 1,890 lbs.; foaled January, 1883; imported 1886; bred by M. Nion, of Coudray-au-Perche, canton of Authon, department of Eure-et-Loir; got by Madere (5308), he by Mouton (1640), he by French Monarch 205 (734), he by Ilderim (5302) (for extension of pedigree see page 27); dam L'Amie (4299) by Madere, he by Coco (belonging to M. Bajeon). A heavy boned, blocky colt, with very level quarters, good disposition, and an easy keeper.

ZEPHYR 5277 (2997).

[Recorded with pedigree in the Percheron Stud Books of France and America.]

Steel grey; 16 hands; weight 1,600 lbs.; foaled April 6, 1883; imported 1886; bred by M. Desire Ducoeurjoly, of La Fontaine, commune of Brunelles, canton of Nogent-le-Rotrou, department of Eure-et-Loir; got by Lyonais 2386 (1332), he by Vaillant (2255), he by Orizaba (belonging to M. Lalouet); dam Perlette (282) by Roland II. (2256), he by Roland I., he by Pamphile (belonging to the Societe Hippique Eure-et-Loir); 2d dam Bichette; 3d dam Pauline (279) by Miramar. A very smooth, stylish, medium sized horse.

We have on hand a number of Grade Stallions and Brood Mares.

IMPORTED AND PURE BRED MARES.

BABETTE 3484.

[Recorded with pedigree in the Percheron Stud Book of America.]

Dark grey ; foaled June, 1885 ; bred at Island Home ; got by Brilliant 1271 (755), he by Brilliant 1899 (756), he by Coco II. (714) (for extension of pedigree see page 27); dam Isis 1744 by Chaldean 854 (637), he by Coco, he by Coco II. (714), etc.; 2d dam Clara Belle 795. Good as Brilliant colts generally are.

CELINA 3685 (2619).

[Recorded with pedigree in the Percheron Stud Books of France and America.]

Black; foaled May 20th, 1881; imported 1884; got by Paul (belonging to M. Caget of Louray), he by Madere (belonging to M. Caget of Almeneches); dam Bijou by Madere (belonging to M. Caget). Broad round hips, clean limbs, wide, deep chest, long bodied, a bright, intelligent face, and a good mover. Dam of Clotilde, and in foal by Pluviose 3755 (683). (For cut see page 56.)

CLOTILDE 5708.

[Recorded with pedigree in the Percheron Stud Book of America.]

Dark grey; foaled Feb. 20th, 1886; bred at Island Home; got by Conquerant 3751 (1798), he by Faisant (belonging to M. Alexander Miard, of Echauffour, department of Orne); dam Celina 3685 (2619), by Paul, he by Madere, dam Bijou by Madere. A remarkably short limbed long bodied filly.

COQUETTE 4170.

[Recorded with pedigree in the Percheron Stud Book of America.]

Steel grey; foaled 1882; got by Romulus 873 (785), he by the Government approved stallion Romulus, he by the Government approved stallion Moreuil; dam Cozette 884 by Selim (749), he by Porthos. A very smooth, stylish mare, like the family she belongs to. In foal by Pluviose 3755 (683).

DRAGONNE 5266 (6558).

[Recorded with pedigree in the Percheron Stud Books of France and America.]

Dapple grey; foaled April 15th, 1881; imported 1886; bred by M. Mauger of Hayes-Barville, commune of Etilleux, canton of Authon, department of Eure-et-Loir; got by Philibert (760), he by Superior 454 (730), he by Favori I. (711), (for extension of pedigree see page 27); dam Malice (6557) by Utopia 780 (731), he by Superior 454 (730), etc. A most excellent brood mare.

ELISE 3869 (2618).

[Recorded with pedigree in the Percheron Stud Books of France and America.]

Grey; foaled May 5th, 1883; imported 1884; got by Vermouth (belonging to M. Miteau), of Genettes, commune of Essai, department of Orne; got by Vermouth (belonging to M. Miteau); dam Mignonne by Solide, belonging to M. Miteau, dam of Troilus 5706, and in foal to Pluviose 3755 (683).

FANCHON 3485.

[Recorded with pedigree in the Percheron Stud Book of America.]

Bay; foaled September, 1885; bred at Island Home; got by Genator (2613), he by Favora 1542 (765), he by French Monarch 205 (734), he by Ilderim (5302) (for extension of pedigree see page 27); dam Nini 3833 (2683) by Passe Partout (1402), he by Comet 104 (719), he by French Monarch 205 (734), etc. A very large smooth filly with a small bright head and pleasant disposition.

VIRGINIE 4169.

GATINE 3683 (2674).

[Recorded with pedigree in the Percheron Stud Books of France and America.]
Black; foaled April 1st, 1884; imported 1884; bred by M. Blot of La Ganase, commune of St. Antoine-de-Rochefort, canton of La Ferte Bernard, department of Sarthe; got by Charlot (belonging to M. Tacheau of La Ferte Bernard), he by Mouton (1640), he by French Monarch 205 (734), he by Ilderim (5302) (for extension of pedigree see page 27); dam Bijou (belonging to M. Blot) by Mouton (1640), etc. Gatine obtained great notoriety in France for her remarkably large arms and stifles, and was parted with only under circumstances of great stress.

HORTENSE 3432.

[Recorded with pedigree in the Percheron Stud Book of America.]
Grey; foaled in 1875; imported in 1881. A very large fine mare and a regular breeder; in foal by Decide (3513).

HORTENSE 5709.

[Recorded with pedigree in the Percheron Stud Book of America.]
Dark grey; foaled July 6th, 1886; bred at Island Home; got by Pluviose 3755 (683), he by Narbonne 1334 (777), he by Brilliant 1899 (756), he by Coco II. (714) (for extension of pedigree see page 27); dam Rosette 3868 (1887) by Madere (1386), he by Brilliant (710), he by Brilliant 1899 (756), etc.; 2d dam Julia (belonging to M. Degout, commune of Condeau, department of Orne.

ISIS 1774.

[Recorded with pedigree in the Percheron Stud Book of America.]
Grey; foaled 1881; bred by H. A. Babcock, Neenah, Wis.; got by Chaldean 637 (854), he by Coco, he by Coco II. (714), (for extension of pedigree see page 27); dam Clara Belle 795 (dam of Babette 3484 and Primus 5705). In foal by Pluviose 3755 (683).

JUBINE 5267 (6559).

[Recorded with pedigree in the Percheron Stud Books of France and America.]
Dapple grey; foaled May 5th, 1882; imported 1886; bred by M. Mauger, of Hayes-de Barville, commune of Etilleux, canton of Authon, department of Eure-et-Loir; got by Favori (447), he by Decide (7304), he by Favori I. (711) (for extension of pedigree see page 27); dam Malice (6557) by Utopia 780 (731), he by Superior 454 (730), he by Favori I. (711), etc.

JULIET 5710.

[Recorded with pedigree in the Percheron Stud Book of America.]
Dark grey; foaled April 10, 1886; bred at Island Home; got by Jupiter 3692 (216), he by Voltaire, he by Monarque, he by Coco II. (714) (for extension of pedigree see page 27); dam Mouvette 2805 (1544) by Madeira 1546 (770), he by Vidocq 483 (732), he by Coco II. (714), etc.; 2d dam by a son of Vidocq 483 (732), etc.

JUNO 891.

[Recorded with pedigree in the Percheron Stud Book of America.]
Grey; foaled 1875; imported 1879; got by Duke de Chartres 162 (721), he by Coco II. (714) (for extension of pedigree see page 27); dam Fleur d'Epine by the Government approved stallion Cheri, he by the Government approved stallion Corbon. A very finely crested, beautiful mare. Dam of Princeps 4166, and in foal by Pluviose 3755 (683).

LA CONTY 5265 (7237).

[Recorded with pedigree in the Percheron Stud Books of France and America.]
Black; foaled April 12, 1881; imported 1886; bred by M. Ferre, of Touches, commune of Souance, canton of Nogent-le-Rotrou, department of Eure-et-Loir; got by Brilliant (710), he by Brilliant 1899 (756), he by Coco II. (714) (for extension of pedigree see page 27); dam Mouton (7236) by Brilliant 63 (718), he by Coco II. (714), etc. A broad, heavy, well finished mare, in foal by Vaillant (404).

MARION 3864 (2682).

[Recorded with pedigree in the Percheron Stud Books of France and America.]

Black; foaled April 5, 1884; imported 1884; bred by M. Mearcelle, of Plisse, commune of Cherreau, canton of La-Ferte-Bernard, department of Sarthe; got by Passe Partout (394), he by Brilliant 1271 (755), he by Brilliant 1899 (756), he by Coco II. (714) (for extension of pedigree see page 27); dam Madelon by Favora 1546 (765), he by French Monarch 205 (734), he by Ilderim (5302) (for extension of pedigree see page 27). Very large for her age, with the markings and characteristics of her grandsire, Brilliant. In foal by Pluviose 3755 (683).

MOUVETTE 2805 (1544).

[Recorded with pedigree in the Percheron Stud Books of France and America.]

Light grey; foaled 1881; imported 1883; bred by M. Th. Goubier, of Berd'huis, canton of Noce, department of Orne; got by Madeira 1546 (770), he by Vidocq 483 (732), he by Coco II. (714) (for extension of pedigree see page 27); dam by a son of Vidocq 483 (732), etc. Good form and action; good feet, and flat legs standing squarely under her body; broad, level hips, deep chest, roomy body, well crested neck, good head, and a capital mover. Dam of Juliet 5710, and in foal by Pluviose 3755 (683).

NINI 3833 (2683).

[Recorded with pedigree in the Percheron Stud Books of France and America.]

Bay; foaled March 7, 1882; imported 1884; bred by M. Rottier, of Berriot, commune of Tuffé, canton of Tuffé, department of Sarthe; got by Passe Partout (1402), he by Comet 104 (719), he by French Monarch 205 (734), he by Ilderim (5302) (for extension of pedigree see page 27); dam Lina by Mouton (1640), he by French Monarch 205 (734), etc. With all the disadvantages of a recent sea voyage, Nini took first premium at the New York State Fair, held at Elmira, September, 1884, not ten days after her arrival. A bright mahogany bay, clean, smooth, and symmetrical throughout, finely crested neck, clean throttle, small clean head well set on, and altogether the finest specimen of the Percheron brood mare we have ever seen. In foal by Pluviose 3755 (683). (For cut see page 52.)

PAOLA 4171.

[Recorded with pedigree in the Percheron Stud Book of America.]

Black; foaled 1883; got by Romulus 873 (785), he by the Government approved stallion Romulus, he by the Government approved stallion Moreuil; dam Fantine 887 by Brilliant 1899 (756), he by Coco II. (714) (for extension of pedigree see page 27); 2d dam by Coco II. (714), etc.

PELOTE 3866 (2622).

[Recorded with pedigree in the Percheron Stud Books of France and America.]

Black; foaled May 25, 1882; imported 1884; bred by M. Jouaux, of Montperoux, commune of Essai, canton of Mesle-sur-Sarthe, department of Orne; got by Lamoureux, he by Favora 1542 (765), he by French Monarch 205 (734), he by Ilderim (5302) (for extension of pedigree see page 27); dam Rosette by Solide, belonging to M. Miteau. Imported with Celina, and a good mate for her, though she will eventually attain a greater weight. Dam of Hector 5707, and in foal by Pluviose 3755 (683).

ROSETTE 3868 (1887).

[Recorded with pedigree in the Percheron Stud Books of France and America.]

Grey; foaled April 20, 1883; imported 1884; bred by M. Degout, commune of Condeau, canton of Regmalard, department of Orne; got by Madere (1386), he by Brilliant (710), he by Brilliant 1899 (756), he by Coco II. (714) (for extension of pedigree see page 27); dam Julie (belonging to M. Degout). Rosette has a fine filly (Hortense 5709), and is in foal by Pluviose 3755 (683).

VIRGINIE 4169.

[Recorded with pedigree in the Percheron Stud Book of America.]

Dapple grey; foaled 1882; got by Romulus 873 (785), he by the Government approved stallion Romulus, he by the Government approved stallion Moreuil; dam Fantine 887 by Brilliant 1899 (756), he by Coco II. (714) (for extension of pedigree see page 27); 2d dam by Coco II. (714), etc. With the beauty of outline and finish of her family, she has great size, excellent action, and is a most beautiful mare. (For cut see page 47.)

NINI 3833 (2683).

DRAFT-HORSES.

The following article appeared in *The Chicago Daily Tribune* of July 16, 1881; and as it demonstrates beyond question the superiority of the Percheron breed over all other races of draft-horses, when crossed upon our native mares, for the production of valuable work animals, we deem it worthy of careful perusal

DRAFT-HORSES—THEIR BREEDING ONE OF THE IMPORTANT INDUSTRIES OF THE DAY— THE EXPERIENCE OF DEALERS WHO BUY AND SELL 40,000 HORSES ANNUALLY— RELATIVE MERITS OF PERCHERON, CLYDESDALE AND ENGLISH HORSES—OPINIONS OF ALL THE LEADING DEALERS IN NEW YORK AND CHICAGO ON THE SUBJECT— THEY ARE UNANIMOUS IN PREFERRING THE FRENCH BREEDS OVER ALL OTHERS— MORE ENDURING, BEST DISPOSITIONED, STAND PAVEMENTS BEST, AND BRING THE HIGHEST PRICES.

The *Tribune*, as the acknowledged champion of the agriculturists of the great Northwest, whose progressive ideas have been established and developed under its tutelage, presents to its readers in this issue a most valuable and timely array of facts bearing upon the relative merits of the different breeds of draft-horses that are being bred in the United States and Canada.

This subject, although of vital importance to the people, is one that, for various causes, has been handled very tenderly by those papers whose duty it is to give the facts to their readers. The agricultural press, which claims to be wholly devoted to the interests of farmers, for fear of losing advertising patronage by publishing that which would injure anybody engaged in handling what is called improved stock, has attempted to pursue a course that would conciliate all. The result has been the mystification of the people, who are at more of a loss what to do than if nothing had been written.

In order that the facts might be known to the people, that they might pursue the most profitable course of breeding, representatives of the *Tribune* were instructed to procure of the well known and leading dealers in the New York and Chicago horse markets information

UPON THE FOLLOWING POINTS:

If they handled draft-horses to any extent, what breeds they handled. Of which particular breed they sold most. Why they sold most of that breed. If the horses of that breed were possessed of more endurance than others. If they had better feet and lasted longer on the city pavements. If they commanded higher prices, or what were the reasons for this particular breed being the favorite. This will account for the similarity of some of the interviews, as, where the gentlemen interviewed did not in their statements cover the several points, these questions were generally propounded.

The result will be of immense value to all those engaged in breeding horses, as well as those who have horses to buy and have not had experience upon which to base their judgment in purchasing. This evidence is of the very best that can be obtained, for it is the accumulated knowledge of years of experience of those who furnish perhaps 40,000 horses annually directly to those who buy them to wear out.

In order to avoid mystifying those persons not versed in the different names often applied to the same breeds, we will explain briefly by stating that those classed as Clydesdales are mostly the produce of horses imported direct from Scotland, or bred in Canada, and imported to the United States. Under the head of English horses are comprised the large Lincolnshire, the Yorkshire, the Suffolk, and other strains.

The French breeds are composed of the Percherons, the Brittany and the Boulonnais. In this country people distinguish them as Percherons, Percheron-Normans, Norman-Percherons, Normans, and French horses. The pure-breds are all recorded, or eligible for entry, in "The Percheron-Norman Stud Book."

The Percherons are considered superior to all the French families, and at the Universal Exposition in 1878, and at all the great shows of France for years, they have carried off the prizes.

The result of the interview was as follows:

ISAAC H. DAHLMAN,

Of 209 and 211 East Twenty-fourth street, New York city, being called upon, requested the scribe to call in the evening, as he was too busy to give any time during the day. In conversation with other dealers it was learned that Mr. I. H. Dahlman is by far the most extensive horse dealer in the New York horse market, and in fact in the country. Nearly all the dealers called upon referred to him as the highest authority on horseflesh.

Calling in the evening, Mr. Dahlman said:

"I handle between 9,000 and 10,000 horses annually on my own account. Do not handle horses on commission for other people. These include all kinds of horses—draft, coach, driving, trotting, and railroad horses. Between 2,500 and 3,000 of these are heavy draft-horses. Of the draft-horses I handle, the great proportion, nearly all, are Percheron-Normans. These Percheron-Norman horses are docile, intelligent, broad between the eyes, and have some brain. They are easily broken, and are steady in harness—meaning that they don't fret when they do their work. They are powerful horses and compactly built—short in the back, deep in the body, and broad in the chest. This gives them what we call 'a good dinner basket.'

"The Norman-Percherons have the best feet of any horse in America. They have a high cup foot. Their feet will stand work on the pavement better than those of any other breed. They are short-coated and thin-skinned, and stand the hot weather the best of any breed. Our heavy draft-horses here have the hardest work in hot weather. The Norman-Percherons generally give the best satisfaction to the people who buy them to wear out. They are very finely developed for their ages. I put them into the heaviest work when four years old, and they stand it. Am buying them as old as I can get, but cannot get them over four years old. I buy these horses because they give the best satisfaction to my customers.

"I don't want it understood that *all* Norman horses have the good qualities. I have seen some imported that were as bad shaped horses as could be found. Some are what I call 'nigger-toed,'—too long in the back and very narrow-waisted. They were not worth their freight from France here. That class of horses is only imported by people who have no judgment in selecting horses—who buy to sell and not to breed. If a man with judgment goes to France to select a stallion or a mare he can find them with the quality.

"A cross on the thoroughbred with a Norman crossed again with a thoroughbred makes a nice coach horse. There is a scarcity of coach horses in this country, and the demand is increasing yearly. It would pay to import some."

Mr. Dahlman was then asked in what respect he considered the Clydesdale horses inferior to the French horses. He said: "I will not give you any criticism on the Clydesdales. I buy very few of them. I prefer to pass his stable and say nothing about him."

Being asked as to the relative prices he was willing to pay for Norman-Percherons and other breeds, Mr. Dahlman said he should have to decline to answer that also, as, if he did, every farmer who owned a Norman horse would want $10 more for him.

He was then asked what breed of horses he would recommend farmers to breed from with reference to selling on the New York market. His answer was that he thought that *The Tribune* readers would understand that from what he had already said.

SOLOMON MEHRBACH,

Of 154 East Twenty-fourth street, New York city, expressed himself as follows:

"I deal largely in all the different kinds of draft-horses—Clydesdales, English and Belgian, and the French horses called Percherous or Normans. Don't know which class I handle most of. Have no preference for either breed, and find that one class of horses sells as well as another. A good horse sells well at any time.

"The Clydes are pretty good horses, but rather flat-footed and slim-waisted."

Mr. Mehrbach then left to attend to some customers, saying that he did not think the western farmers needed any information on the subject of horse-breeding.

Returning the next day, and pressing Mr. Mehrbach for more information, he said: "Have you seen Mr. I. H. Dahlman?" The reporter said he had. "Well, he likes the Normans, don't he?" "Yes." "Well. I like the Clydes. I handle more of them than I do of the Normans. They give better satisfaction to my customers, have more bone, better feet and last longer. They have more action than the Normans."

A. S. CHAMBERLIN,

Of 147 East Twenty-fourth street, New York city, runs what are known as "the Old

CELINA 3685 (2619).

Bull's Head" stables. He has been longer in the stable business than any man in New York city, having been so engaged for upward of forty years. Mr. C. said:

"I keep exchange and sale stables for horses. Don't deal on my own account to any extent. All classes of horses, amounting to several thousands annually, come to my stables from all sections of the country. A large number of these are draft horses of the different breeds, the Clydesdales, the French horses called Percherons or Normans, the English and Belgian. There seems to be a larger demand for the French horses than for any other breed.

"Some years ago we used to get a great many horses from Upper Canada. These were Clydesdales, and would weigh from 1,400 to 1,600 pounds, but they did not seem to answer the purpose; as a general thing their feet were thin-shelled and flat, and being heavy horses their feet would become sore and would not stand the pavements. The French horses have good feet and stand the pavements better than the Clydesdales. That is the reason they sell better. The Norman horses are the finest looking and most attractive; have better action, are quicker stepping horses, and stand their work better than the Clydes. The Norman horse brings a better price on the market.

"The Clydesdales are heavy-boned, heavy-limbed horses, strong in the shoulder, and strong-hipped. They are, however, short-ribbed, slim-waisted, and lack action. Comparatively few Clydesdales are now brought to this market. Either they don't raise them, or don't bring them to this market. The demand is largely for the Norman horses.

"I would advise the farmers and breeders who are breeding horses to sell on the New York market for draft purposes to breed from the French horses in preference to all others."

OAKLEY & SMITH,

Of 160 East Twenty-fourth street, New York city, were seen. Mr. Oakley said:

"Our firm handles several thousand horses annually, and upward of a thousand of them are heavy draft horses. We handle all kinds of heavy horses, Clydesdales, English and Belgian, and the French horses called Percherons or Normans. We handle rather more of the Clydesdales than of the other breeds. We handle those horses we can get the easiest. There is no greater demand for the Clydesdales than for other breeds. The Clydesdales are generally a little short in the rib and light-waisted, but have good shoulders and rumps.

"I don't see much difference in the feet of the different breeds, or their wearing qualities. The Normans are good stocky horses, compactly built. Still, when I see a horse I like, I pay little attention to the breed."

Mr. Oakley was then asked what class of horses he would advise the farmers and breeders of the country to breed to with reference to raising horses for the New York market. He replied; "A cross of the Norman horse on our native mares would be my choice, and that is the sort of breeding I would recommend."

JACOB DAHLMAN

Of 207 East Twenty-fourth street, New York city, said:

"I handle on my own account between 1,500 and 1,800 horses annually. This includes all kinds of horses, but a large proportion of them are heavy horses of the various large breeds, the French horses called Percheron-Normans, Clydesdales, English and Belgian.

"I handle a great many of the Percheron-Norman horses, more of them than of any other breed. There is more demand for them than for any other class. The French horses are the best, have the best feet, last longer on New York pavements, and always give satisfaction. They are more compactly built, there is more work in them, and they are better broken. They have better action than the other breeds.

"The Clydesdales are next thing to the Norman horses. They are very good horses. I have handled a good many of them, but there are not many of them on the market nowadays. As to prices, anything in the way of a good blocky horse, built like a Norman, with good bone and good feet, will bring the same price as a Norman horse.

"I would advise the farmers and breeders who are breeding horses with reference to selling on the New York market, to breed from the Percheron-Norman horses in preference to any other breed.

C. & H. HAYMAN,

Of 213 and 215 East Twenty-fourth street, New York city, were also seen. Mr. H. Hayman said:

"We handle about 2,000 horses a year, principally heavy draft. We handle all kinds of large horses raised in this country, including Clydesdales, the French horses, English and Belgian. We handle more of the Normans than of the others. Have more demand for them than for the other breeds. The people like them better, and they bring higher prices than the other breeds. The Norman horses have the best feet, and last better on the New York pavements. They have the most endurance, and generally give good satisfaction. The Norman horse is more easily broken, and is the best dispositioned horse we have. Norman horses mature sooner, and are ready for the market when much younger than those of other breeds.

"The Clydesdales are open-made horses, not so compact and well-finished as the French horses. The Clydesdales are not only not so well shaped, but their feet are not so good as those of the Normans.

"We would advise the farmers and breeders of the West to breed to Norman horses in preference to any other breed with a view to selling on the New York market."

A. M. STEIN & CO.,

Of 229 Washington street, Brooklyn, N. Y., were seen. Mr. D. W. Stein said:
"We have been in the business over twenty years. We handle nearly 2,000 head of horses annually. Large numbers of them are heavy draft horses. We handle all kinds, the Clydesdales, the French horses called Percherons, English and Belgian. We handle more of the Percheron-Normans than of any other breed. There is more demand for them. They give the best satisfaction, no matter how little of the blood there is in them. Generally they have good feet and last better on our pavements than the Clydesdales, or any of the other breeds. The Belgian horse is a good horse.

"The Percheron-Norman horse has the best action of any breed, and, weight and condition being equal, brings the highest price in the market.

"The Clydesdales haven't as good a foot, haven't as good action, nor as much rib nor as broad a breast as the Percheron-Normans. Neither are they as good feeders. Take a Percheron-Norman and a Clydesdale, each in poor condition, and feed them alike for two months, and the Percheron-Norman will improve 200 per cent. more than the Clydesdale. The only trouble with the Percheron-Normans is their scarcity. Tell the farmers of the West to keep their Percheron-Norman mares and breed them. I would advise them to breed from Percheron-Norman horses in preference to any other breed for the purpose of selling on this market."

Mr. Stein has made quite a study of breeding horses. He has spent some time in France, and seemed quite well posted as to the French methods of breeding.

HENRY NEWMAN,

Of 328 Rutledge street, Brooklyn, was not at home when the reporter called, but his son, Mr. P. Newman, said:
"We handle a large number of horses of all kinds. A good many are heavy draft. We are handling mostly French-Canadian horses, but get some from Ohio and Indiana. We handle more French horses than of any other breed. They give better satisfaction than the Clydesdales and other breeds. They have better feet, and last longer on our pavements, and bring better prices than any other class of horses. We have more demand for them, and they give satisfaction generally. They are more compactly built than the Clydesdales. We don't like the long-geared horses.

"We would advise the farmers to breed from French horses to sell on this market in preference to any other breed."

S. RICHEY,

Of 341 Rutledge street, Brooklyn, said:
"I handle a large number of horses, principally heavy draft. This includes all of the heavy breeds, Clydesdales, English, Belgian, and the French horses called Normans. I handle about the same number of each, I think. The Normans are compactly-built horses, and have more wear in them than the other breeds of horses. They are not so large. The Norman horses have the best feet. I think the reason is on account of their coming from the West, where they don't have to shoe them so young, and the soil seems to agree with their feet. Their action, too, seems to be as good as that of the other breeds. I think the Clydesdales or English horses are the most showy, have more size and stand up higher. The Normans are more compact, lower built, shorter necked—are workers.

"The Clydesdales have more white marks about them—more white faces and white on their fore legs than the other breeds, and that hurts them for this market.

"The prevailing color of the Norman horses is gray, and a matched pair of grays will bring more money than any other color. The Normans are better selling horses, and give the best satisfaction of any of the breeds to customers. If I were buying for my own use I would have nothing but the Normans. I would advise the farmers and breeders to breed Norman horses in preference to any others with a view of selling on this market."

A. J. HEINEMAN,

Of Mansfield, Ohio, was seen. Mr. Heineman said:

"I handle about 2,000 horses a year, principally heavy draft horses, and ship altogether to the New York market. I handle all kind of draft horses, including the Percheron-Normans, Clydesdales, Belgian and English breeds.

"I handle more of the Norman horses because there is more demand for them, and they are the best draft horses we have. After the Normans the Belgians are the best, and next to them the English.

"The Normans have more body, are finer looking, and are better movers than the other breeds. They have better feet than the Clydesdales, and better ends, broad breasts and rumps. The Normans are better dispositioned horses than the Clydesdales. The brewers of New York, as a general thing, will not buy a Clydesdale horse, on account of his feet and disposition. We can't sell one Clydesdale where we can sell 100 Normans. The Clydesdales are narrow-waisted, as a general thing, and cannot stand what a Norman can. When a Clydesdale horse gets sick he goes to pieces quicker than any other class of horses. The Clydesdales have no constitutions.

"I would give $50 more for a good Norman or Belgian horse than I will for a Clydesdale, condition and weight being equal. A cross of Norman and Clydesdale makes a very good horse.

"I would advise farmers and breeders to breed to Norman and Belgian horses in preference to any other breed, with reference to selling on the New York market."

F. J. BERRY,

10 Monroe street, Chicago, has sold about 600 horses since the first of last January, and handles all kinds of horses—French, Clydesdales, English and Belgian. Said Mr. Berry:

"I sell more of the Normans than of any other breed, because they are sought after more than the others. They are possessed of more endurance than the others; ship better, are better feeders, and for all purposes are far superior to all other horses now raised. The half or three-fourths grades are better for heavy draft, while the lower grades come in for all use. From one-eighth to one-fourth grades make the best driving horses and have splendid action, are finely developed, and have good style; they are all well flanked down.

"They have better feet than the Clydesdales, and last on our pavements fully as well as any horses we have.

"As to Clydesdales, they, as a general thing, are good feeders. They have the very best bone, and are large, rugged horses. The objection to them is, they are light in the flank, and a little long in the back, ship poorly, and draw up in the flank. They are a big improvement over the common horse, and the next best thing to the Normans. The Normans have good action and are fair roadsters, and bring better prices than the other breeds.

"I would advise every farmer to breed to French horses in preference to any other, and I am surprised that farmers and breeders of horses pay so little attention to the kind of horses they breed, when they can breed Norman horses that will bring in the market, when four or five years old, from $150 to $300 a head. I used to be prejudiced against the French horses before I had handled them extensively, but now I am convinced that for all purposes there is nothing equal to the grade Norman."

MICHIGAN CENTRAL

Passenger Station, foot of Third Street, as follows:

In Effect November 28th, 1886.

Leave.	NORTHWARD.	Arrive.
† 7.05 A.M.	D., L. & N. Express for Petoskey and Mackinaw	† 9.45 P.M.
† 8.35 "	M. C. Express for Saginaw & Bay City, with Parlor Car	† 9.00 "
† 8.30 "	F. & P. M. Bay City, Saginaw and Way Mail, with Parlor Car	† 10.35 A.M.
† 9.55 "	D., L. & N. Express and Mail for Big Rapids and Howard City	† 3.45 P.M.
† 1.10 P.M.	F. & P. M. Bay City, Saginaw and Ludington Express, with Parlor Car	† 3.50 "
† 5.00 "	D., L. & N. Greenville Express	† 11.50 A.M.
† 5.30 "	F. & P. M. Express for Bay City and Saginaw, with Parlor Car	† 10.00 P.M.
† 5.40 "	M. C. Express for Bay City, Saginaw and Mackinaw, with Sleeping Car	† 11.10 A.M.
‡ 11.00 "	M. C. Express for Bay City and Saginaw, with Sleeping Car	† 6.05 "
* 11.30 "	F. & P. M. Bay City, Saginaw and Ludington Express, with Sleeper	† 2.45 "

SOUTHWARD.

† 8.25 A.M.	M. C. Express for Toledo, Cincinnati and Indianapolis, with Parlor Cars	† 8.10 A.M.
* 3.00 P.M.	M. C. Express for Toledo, Columbus and St. Louis, with Parlor Cars	* 11.40 "
† 5.05 "	M. C. Grosse Ile Accommodation	† 8.00 "
† 7.20 "	M. C. Express for Toledo and the South, with Cincinnati Sleeper	† 5.25 P.M.
* 9.00 "	M. C. Express for Toledo and the South, with Cleveland Sleeper	* 10.50 "

EASTWARD.

† 5.00 A.M.	M. C. Mail for Way Stations to Buffalo	* 8.45 P.M
* 6.10 "	M. C. Atlantic Express, with Sleepers for New York and Boston and Dining Car to Buffalo	* 8.45 "
* 12.05 P.M.	M. C. Express for Buffalo, with Sleepers for New York and Boston	¶ 5.20 "
† 7.15 "	M. C. Express for Buffalo, New York and Boston, with Syracuse Sleepers	* 8.05 A.M.
* 10.55 "	M. C. Limited New York Express, with Sleepers for Toronto, Buffalo, Boston and New York and Dining Car to Rochester	* 1.05 P.M.

WESTWARD.

† 7.00 A.M.	M. C. Mail for Chicago and Way Stations, via Mail Line	† 6.00 P.M.
† 9.10 "	M. C. Day Express for Chicago, Grand Rapids and Muskegon Parlor Car	† 6.45 "
* 1.30 P.M.	M. C. Fast Western Express for Chicago, Sleeping and Dining Cars	* 10.45 "
† 4.00 "	M. C. Express for Jackson, Grand Rapids and Kalamazoo	† 11.45 A.M.
* 8.00 "	M. C. Evening Express for Chicago, with Sleeping Cars	* 7.30 "
* 9.15 "	M. C. Pacific Express for Chicago, with Sleepers for Chicago and Grand Rapids and Dining Car to Chicago	* 6.00 "

* Daily. † Except Sunday. ‡ Except Saturday. ¶ Except Monday.

NOTE.—This Passenger Station is occupied by the Michigan Central, Detroit, Lansing & Northern and Flint & Pere Marquette Railroads exclusively.

D. EDWARDS,
Asst. Gen. Mngr. F. & P. M. R. R., East Saginaw.

O. W. RUGGLES,
Gen. Pass. & Tkt. Agt. M. C. R. R., Chicago.

W. A. CARPENTER.
Traffic Mngr. D. L. & N. R. R., Detroit.

CHARLES A. WARREN,
Union Pass. & Tkt. Agt., 66 Wood. av. cor. Jeff. and ft. 3d st.